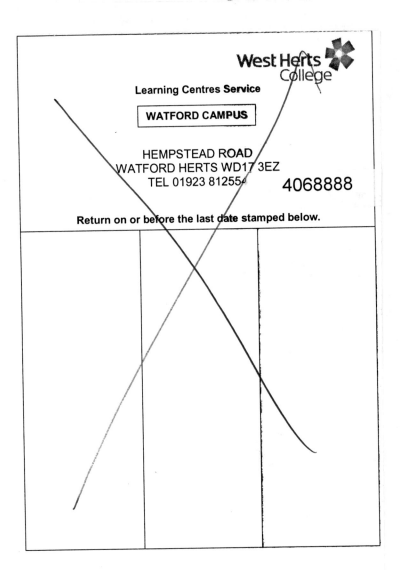

West Herts
College

Learning Centres **Service**

WATFORD CAMPUS

HEMPSTEAD ROAD
WATFORD HERTS WD17 3EZ
TEL 01923 812554   4068888

Return on or before the last date stamped below.

WATFORD LRC

LIGHTING TECHNIQUES FOR THEATRE IN-THE-ROUND

Jackie Staines

ENTERTAINMENT TECHNOLOGY PRESS

Application & Techniques Series

For Robin who has brought me love and laughter.
For Archie, Ava and Lily-Mae.

The book must also be dedicated in memory of Stephen Joseph
since none of this would have been possible
without him; and also to Sir Alan Ayckbourn for
continuing the artistic and technical developments – and the
enthusiasm – for theatre-in-the-round in Great Britain.

LIGHTING TECHNIQUES FOR THEATRE-IN-THE-ROUND

Jackie Staines

Foreword by Sir Alan Ayckbourn

Entertainment Technology Press

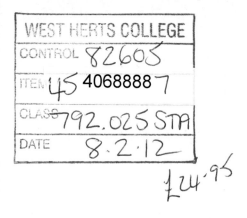

Lighting Techniques For Theatre-In-The-Round

© Jackie Staines

First publication October 2000

A title in continuous publication within the
Entertainment Technology Press Application & Techniques Series

Published by Entertainment Technology Press Ltd
The Studio, High Green, Great Shelford, Cambridge, CB22 5EG
Internet: www.etnow.com

LTTR / 008_08_10

FOREWORD
Sir Alan Ayckbourn

I suppose I'm the suitable person to write this foreword to Jackie's excellent book. I am, after all, the director who set her the bulk of the problems which she faced (and successfully solved) during her years as Chief Technician / Lighting Designer at the Scarborough Stephen Joseph Theatre at Westwood.

Working in the Round presents its own challenges as well as benefits. Many of these land on the designers' desks – to dream up sets that don't obscure actors but can nonetheless convey complex information – multiple locations that can be suggested by atmospheric light alone but which still ensure that the actor remains lit.

Stephen Joseph, rogue man of theatre, innovator and revolutionary had a profound influence on me and through me on virtually anyone who works in our theatre. Sooner or later they are bound to come face to face with one of the so-called Stephen Joseph Maxims. These were numerous, sometimes sweeping and generalised, occasionally even contradictory. All theatres should be built to self destruct within seven years, is one I try to live by. Simplified, what that means to me is that every few years those entrusted with running our theatres should seek new ways, new approaches to their art and programming. They should not be afraid to start afresh.

Another, equally important Maxim and at the very core of his theatre-in-the-round doctrine was that theatre, essentially, consisted of two elements. Actor and Audience. All other disciplines, though he was careful not to dismiss them, were supportive. Writer, director, designer, technician, stage manager should understand that they are there to enable this event, the meeting between the watcher and the performer. Never, never to come between it.

Yet how often have we seen performers virtually eclipsed by scenery or forced into costumes which restrict their smallest movement. How often sat through a production lit in such Stygian gloom that not an expression, not a gesture can be discerned. I once appeared in a production of *A Man For All Seasons* where the only light on stage was a blue downlight to indicate the river Thames. The banks were by contrast in total darkness. Exasperated, I finally took to the water to gain some light, explaining to the director that there was no historical record that Sir Thomas More was <u>not</u> a first rate swimmer. The latest enemy to performers is the over ambitious supplier of sound effects anxious to show off a new ring of 2000 ohm speakers.

What Jackie's book demonstrates, besides providing a supremely practical handbook for anyone setting out to light in-the-round, is that lighting is just one of the key servants of the performance. A contributor, an enabler. Also, in the Round's case, it is an invaluable element in the creation of seamless story telling.

The regular designer of my new plays, Mick Hughes, best summed it up when I once asked if there was a chance that a lamp could be angled a bit further on-stage for a particular moment, that is if he didn't mind me suggesting it. He shrugged. "All my lights are whores," he replied, "They'll go with anyone."

Scarborough
September 2000

CONTENTS

INTRODUCTION 11

1 WHO WAS STEPHEN JOSEPH? 13

2 DESIGNING GENERAL COVER 25
Two Cover, or Not Two Cover? 32
What is Backlight Anyway? 33
Using Sections and Elevations. 37
Using Colour in the General Cover 40

3 HOW SPECIAL ARE SPECIALS? 47
What is Keylight in-the-round? 47
Effects, Pyrotechnics, and Smoke 52

4 PAINTING THE STAGE 55
Lighting for fun 57
Lighting for Darkness 61
Using The Floor As A Canvas 67

5 NIGHTMARES FROM ROUND STREET 71
Patching Large Rigs 71
Finding Enough Positions 72
Gobo Washes Galore 76
Grid Obstacles 77
Size Isn't Everything 79
Floor Surfaces 82
Practicals and Problems 84
Flying Pieces and Tall Actors 96
Walls, Stairs, and Voms 99
The Beauty Of Symmetry 102

6 LIGHTING DESIGNS IN THE ROUND......................107
   Design Examples From Others 107
   Mick Hughes, Lighting Designer 107
   Kath Geraghty, Senior Technician:
       Stephen Joseph Theatre..110
   David Taylor; Lighting Designer and
       Theatre Consultant..116
   Jo Dawson, Chief Electrician and Lighting Designer;
       New Victoria Theatre, Newcastle-Under-Lyme..............124

7 REMEMBRANCE...135

Appendix 1 Planning For New Theatre Forms............139

Appendix 2 Index of Photographs and Diagrams........149

Appendix 3 Resume of Design Examples......................153

Appendix 4 'Round' Venues..161

Appendix 5 Bibliography and Further Reading............165

ACKNOWLEDGEMENTS

The creation of this book would have been impossible without the help and contributions from the following:

Sir Alan Ayckbourn: Playwright and Director
Sue Condie: Set Designer and Photographer
Jo Dawson: Chief Electrician and Lighting Designer
Adrian Gatie: Production Photographer
Kath Geraghty: Technician and Lighting Designer
John Haynes: Photographer
Mick Hughes: Lighting Designer
Strand Lighting Ltd
David I Taylor: Lighting Designer and Theatre Consultant
Bob Watson: Stephen Joseph Theatre Librarian

INTRODUCTION

I was indeed very flattered when Entertainment Technology Press asked me to write a book on lighting theatre-in-the-round, although I was a little taken aback as I have spent much of my time recently working on the development of lighting control rather than lighting design.

For that reason I decided to make this a technical volume as part of the **Application & Techniques** series, rather than a book about design, although I have of course included several design examples.

These have come mainly from my seven years at the Stephen Joseph Theatre in Scarborough, but also from the contributions of other lighting designers working in the same staging format.

I felt very strongly that any book about theatre-in-the-round should pay suitable homage to Stephen Joseph, and it is with great thanks to Sir Alan Ayckbourn for giving me an informal anecdotal interview that I am able to include a chapter dedicated to Stephen Joseph and his pioneering ideas.

My intention is that the reader will find this book a useful reference source when working as a lighting designer in theatre-in-the-round for the first time. It also provides some anecdotes and ideas for more intricate shows, and attempts to blow away some of the myths that have been written about lighting theatre-in-the-round.

Theatre-in-the-round can be challenging, but also extremely rewarding. However, once used to designing 'in-the-round', moving back to proscenium stages often requires considerable readjustment. Theatre-in-the-round is a very natural staging format, and a return to the proscenium format can seem somewhat false. However, theatre-in-the-round offers plenty of opportunity for good fun lighting as well as pure naturalism.

Jackie Staines,
Cambridge,
September 2000.

1 WHO WAS STEPHEN JOSEPH?

Stephen Joseph, born to Michael Joseph the publisher and the actress Hermione Gingold on 13th June 1921, was "perhaps the most successful missionary to work in the theatre since the Second World War"[1]. Early reports suggest that his interest in theatre may have begun during his public school education at Claysmore in Dorset, which was cut short by his acceptance to attend the Central School of Speech and Drama at the age of 16.

Although he began working in theatre immediately after leaving college, his early theatrical career was stalled by the onset of World War II. He joined the war effort as a member of the Royal Navy, and received two medals for bravery, one of which was earned by rescuing the ship's puppy when it fell overboard!

After the war, he continued his studies at Cambridge University where he dedicated himself to the activities of the Footlights Revue Company, if not wholly to his studies. As well as acting, he was also directing, writing, and designing shows. His enthusiasm was not only for the productions themselves, but also for making economic use of limited resources, and it was this philosophy that was the starting point for many of his future theories and methods.

Although he had seen one amateur production performed in a theatre-in-the-round format, it was a college exchange visit to the United States that provided the influence for him to pioneer theatre-in-the-round in Great Britain. Of that very first performance, he said:

> *"... when I saw this production of 'A Phoenix Too Frequent'*
> *in-the-round I was delighted at the simplicity of the lighting and*
> *staging, and the natural and easy way the actors set about their task."*

After a few years in various teaching appointments, Stephen Joseph eventually realised his dream when he found a suitable building that could accommodate an arena stage performance space. It followed a drama course at Wrea Head in the North Riding of Yorkshire when the organiser, John Wood arranged for him to visit the concert room of Scarborough public library. It was a large room: about 50ft x 40ft, and 24ft high[2]. *"Why not stage your plays here?"*

---

[1] From *The Times* obituary for Stephen Joseph published in October 1967.

Joseph reacted with a mixture of joy and panic. Here was a room that could be converted into a temporary theatre-in-the-round. Backstage space was limited, lighting would be difficult, and special scaffolding platforms would have to be erected to raise the seating. It was a possible but daunting project. It was easy to dream but difficult to take the responsibility for putting those dreams into practice. Finance was also a problem, but somewhat alleviated by the help of the redoubtable Ken Boden (General Manager, Scarborough Theatre Trust providing voluntary front-of-house-staff and various fund raising schemes.

Thus theatre-in-the-round was born in Scarborough and during the same period, Stephen Joseph managed a series of Sunday night experimental plays performed in-the-round in the hall of the Mahatma Ghandi building in London, using actors from the casts of long running West End shows.

The press announcement for the very first theatre-in-the-round season in Great Britain was made in 1955 and read:

"Theatre shows at which the audience will sit on all sides of the stage, will open at Scarborough on July 14th, for two months. The entertainment, "Theatre-in-the-round" presented by Mr. Stephen Joseph, 34 year old son of miss Hermione Gingold, will be given in the concert room at the Public Library. A lecturer at the Central School of Speech and Drama in London, and a Cambridge graduate, Mr. Joseph intends to manage the non-profit making Studio Theatre Company. The company, with 10 players, will present four new plays by English playwrights. Productions will run from Thursday to Tuesday. This will give holidaymakers a chance to see two different plays in one week.

It will be the first time the experiment has been tried in Britain. The arts council is taking a keen interest in it. Mr. Joseph said that he had seen the entertainment in the U.S. and it gave actors excellent training for film and T.V. work, apart from enabling an enormous cut in costs. He added: "Many people who watch films and T.V. will not normally go to the theatre, but this type of theatre may appeal to them. With lower costs we can try to present entirely new plays which the normal theatre would not do." The concert hall will have 248 seats and the arena stage will be 14ft by 18ft[3].

This new performance format caused great consternation amongst the local theatre-going community, who had never witnessed anything quite so radical

---

[2]   15m x 12m x 7m
[3]   4m x 5.5m

before, and often not particularly 'warm' towards its intimacy and lack of scenery.

Letters were published in the local press both for and against the theatre, but as the old adage goes: "No publicity is bad publicity", and the debate may have drawn the necessary attention to the theatre in its early days and helped to secure its future:

> *Sir: One factor of the utmost importance: Theatre-in-the-round has no settings. How can any modern audience, conditioned to the detailed scenic designs of film and television, be expected to enjoy a play performed in limbo?*
>
> *When, as in the current production, I note from the theatre programme that the action of a play is to take place in a living room, I expect to see a living room, with doors that open and shut. If the social status of the residents is sufficiently high, wallpaper does not come a miss. Yet here we are presented with a miscellany of furniture, and expected to use our imaginations!*
>
> *To enter a theatre and to be told to create the décor for ourselves is equivalent to entering a restaurant, being presented with a dish of raw vegetables, and being told to imagine the cooking. The directors of theatre-in-the-round have only themselves to blame if the audience, cheated of spectacle, prefers to spend its shillings on the latest CinemaScope epic. – Yours etc. Reginald Cooper.[4]*
>
> *Sir: Judging by the views of your correspondents in recent letters, it seems that the essential meaning and purpose of this new form of dramatic representation in the Library Theatre has escaped the notice of too many people.*
>
> *Theatre-in-the-round attempts to transport the audience right into the action of the play and capture the interest of the individual by its proximity. Décor, of necessity, is laid aside. But it is more than compensated for by the vivid nature of the presentation. Surely the plot of a drama and the high standard of acting and production are sufficient to make us forget about such negligible details as wall-paper? I cannot agree that such an intellectually and spiritually satisfying enter-tainment is comparable with an uncooked meal. The simile is entirely out of proportion.*

---

[4] Letter published in the *Scarborough Evening News*, 1st August 1955.

In an age pampered by the artificial luxuriance of scenic spectacle it is refreshing to find this new form of art, which appeals to the inner and deeper feelings, and in this lies its chief claim to superiority. – Yours, etc. Christopher J. Woodland.[5]

Photograph 1: Stephen Joseph

A stir in the arts world, or Stephen Joseph simply generating his own publicity material? The editor of the newspaper closed this correspondence with the realisation that Stephen Joseph himself may well have been responsible for writing both letters!

During the first season at the Library Theatre in Scarborough, the stage was illuminated by eight spotlights; one in each corner of the room, and one on each side. This small rig illuminated the acting area but provided little more than the ability to fade the lights up and down.

Lighting as a design concept was not a major consideration in those days, and it was left to the actors to make sure that they found 'somewhere bright' to stand whilst delivering important speeches! In the following season, this 'rig' was enhanced by the provision of corner brackets and cableways through the roof void. The lighting was controlled by a 'Junior 8' type resistance dimmer installation.

Lighting in the early days of theatre-in-the-round was of necessity very basic. It was as much to do with lack of resources as with lack of inclination. Stephen Joseph was very much a purist and believed that theatre was for actors and writers, although he became one of the first directors to use recorded sound on tape in the theatre. However, at this point he began to think more 'technically' and to develop a taste for the possibilities of sound and lighting effects.

When the rig at the Library Theatre increased to 16 luminaires, he became increasingly more interested in the 'How–To' of theatre lighting, and of lighting this particular staging format. At this time he began documenting his staging and lighting techniques, and became concerned about the design of new theatres of all types.

---

[5] Letter published in the *Scarborough Evening News* 2nd August 1955.

THEATRE IN THE ROUND

Photograph 2: Postcard of The Library Theatre Scarborough circa 1958 had a basic lighting rig of just 16 luminaires.

Stephen Joseph was a founder member of the Association of British Theatre Technicians (ABTT) in 1961:

> *"... whose main purpose is to raise technical standards in the theatre by collecting and making available information concerning theatre planning, stage machinery, lighting and sound equipment, acoustic, scenery construction, stage management and all aspects of presentation. The Association provides a forum for discussion among theatre technicians through the publication of a newsletter and through regular meetings ... the Association is not a trade union nor does it confer on members any professional status."*

He was also a driving force behind the Society of Theatre Consultants and wrote many essays, articles, and books on the subject of planning new theatres on behalf of both of these organisations.

The diagram shown in *Figure 1* above, is an original sketch by Stephen Joseph of 'an ideal control room layout'. It clearly shows from left to right: a two preset manual lighting control, a prompt desk, two reel-to-reel tape decks with operating position and mixer in between, and space for

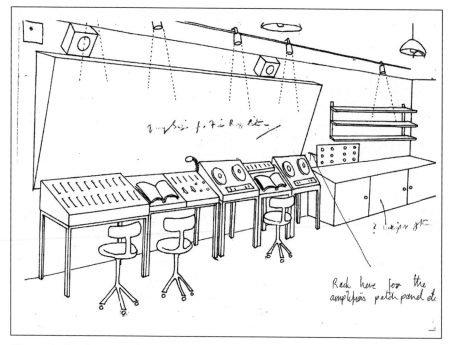

Figure 1: Stephen Joseph's Control Room Design.

amplifiers and sound patch facilities. Lost from this diagram, but in the same archive material is the reference to the lighting hard patch located behind the lighting operator's position. This basic design was used in the Westwood building at Scarborough until additional dimmers were installed and the patch bay had to move. A visitor to that building today (which is now used by the East Yorkshire Coast College) would be able to see a distinct similarity between the actual control room and the drawing.

As the lighting rig at the Scarborough Library Theatre grew, so did Stephen Joseph's methods and theories, although putting ideas into practice was often restricted by lack of resources.

It was during these early Scarborough years that the '120° rule' was established as an acceptable method of lighting theatre-in-the-round, whilst avoiding the necessary rig size caused by lighting from all four sides. This method allows the use of three instruments per lighting area instead of four, which results in fewer instruments being tied up for general illumination and more made available for 'specials'.

Photograph 3: A performance of 'Just Between Ourselves' at Scarborough's Library Theatre in 1976, showing the scaffolding grid and a larger quantity of luminaires.

As the seasons at the Library grew, wall brackets were no longer adequate and some a scaffolding grid had to be designed. The first grid was designed to be mobile to enable the same lighting equipment to be toured into different venues. It consisted of upright scaffolding poles in each corner of the room, with cross bars adjoining each corner. The original construction was highly unstable and was soon redesigned. The replacement construction consisted of towers that were placed behind the seating blocks and were unable to fall in any direction. By the mid-seventies standing structures were replaced by a suspended construction that was capable of accommodating a much larger lighting rig.

The last performance at Scarborough Library Theatre was of Alan Ayckbourn's *Just Between Ourselves* in 1976, and was lit by a far larger rig than the original eight spotlights, or come to that, any of Stephen Joseph's early lighting ideas.

During the early years of the Library Theatre in Scarborough, it was Stephen

Photograph 4: Alan Ayckbourn (left) and John Smith circa 1957 await their respective sound and lighting cues.

Joseph who pioneered many of the lighting and sound techniques, but the rigging and operation of all things technical was left to the young acting ASM: Alan Ayckbourn.

Ayckbourn worked at the Library Theatre as acting ASM from 1957 onwards, and began writing when he was disillusioned with the parts he was being cast in. The sarcastic comment by Stephen Joseph suggesting that the young actor should write his own parts in future led to the career path of one of our greatest-ever playwrights.

Despite the early death of Stephen Joseph in 1967, the company continued to perform in the Library Theatre each summer until 1976, when it moved to a specially adapted venue within Scarborough's former boys' high school, and the company was renamed *Theatre In The Round At Westwood.*

The initial conversion of the school hall to an almost purpose-designed theatre-in-the-round cost in the region of £40,000 and was only designed to last three years. The seating risers were of a wooden construction and the seats themselves salvaged from another refurbishment programme. Lighting positions were provided by a series of parallel internally wired bars installed

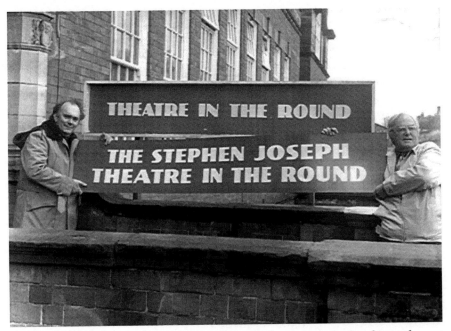

Photograph 5: Alan Ayckbourn (left) and Ken Boden rename the Scarborough theatre in 1978

across the ceiling of the theatre. There were 122 grid height outlets, and a further six outlets at stage floor level, wired back to 40 x JTM wall-mounted dimmers via a patch bay, and controlled by a Strand JP40 console.

By the mid-eighties, an extra 20 ways of STM dimmers had been added and control was by a Strand Gemini. More scaffolding bars were placed at right angles to the original IWBs[6], which over the years eventually completed a grid based roughly on 1.5m squares. There were 128 socket outlets patched back to the 60 JTM and STM dimmers, and access to the grid was by stepladders as there was very little height above the bars.

By the mid 1990s all of Stephen Joseph's basic rules and techniques had not only been broken, but positively decimated by myself and other lighting designers and technicians working in that venue – not because Stephen Joseph was wrong, but because modern technology allows much greater freedom for the lighting designer. In fact, a busy repertory season still relies on a standard

---

[6] IWB = Internally Wired Bar

'general rig' to illuminate the acting area, to which specials are added for each show. The fun comes in with the quantity of luminaires available, and the sophistication of the control system.

The Westwood building was renamed as 'The Stephen Joseph Theatre' when the lease on the building was extended in 1978. By this time, Alan Ayckbourn had taken the title of 'Director of Productions' for the Stephen Joseph Theatre Company, as well as establishing himself as a prolific playwright. A two year sabbatical at the National Theatre, and a knighthood later, Sir Alan Ayckbourn is Artistic Director of the company to this day.[7] Ken Boden continued to work in administration for the Scarborough Theatre Trust (the charitable funding body of the Stephen Joseph Theatre Company) until the late eighties when illness forced his retirement. He died in February 1991.

Photograph 6:
Sir Alan Ayckbourn.
Photograph by John Haynes

The Stephen Joseph Theatre company remained in the 'Westwood' building until 1996 when it moved to its current home in the former Odeon cinema in Scarborough, hereinafter referred to as 'Westborough'. Lighting facilities were upgraded to 240 (yes, from 60 to 240) dimmers, controlled by an ADB Vision10 control desk. In the new venue, access to the lighting equipment was radically improved by the inclusion at the design stage of a 'tension-wire grid' – a sort of steel wire 'trampoline' that technical staff can walk over, and the luminaires light through. This system was already being used in Canada, but this was the first installation of its type in the United Kingdom. Another technical enhancement that was included at the design stage of the 'Odeon Conversion' was a full size stage lift and 'slip stages' that allow the repertory sets to be moved easily between stage, rehearsal room, and workshop. The building also has a meeting room named in honour of the late Ken Boden.

Sir Alan Ayckbourn feels that Stephen Joseph would thoroughly approve of

---

[7] September 2000

the technical and artistic advances made both at the Westwood building and at Westborough – advances that have been made possible by the provision of many more luminaires and dimmers than he ever imagined, the plethora of colour and special effects made available to today's designers, and the improved accessibility to the lighting equipment for rigging and focusing.

2 DESIGNING GENERAL COVER

Designing General Cover

Before getting involved in the artistic requirements of a show, the first job is to illuminate the actors wherever they are on the stage. To achieve this, the McCandless 45° rule can be simply adapted to suit viewing positions from all sides, not just the 'front', thus resulting in four luminaires per acting area at a 90 degree separation from each other.

The disadvantage of this method is that it will quickly eat into the resources of the available equipment, leaving the designer with few luminaires and circuits for specials. This situation can become very disheartening to a designer faced with an exciting show, so methods of 'cheating' must be devised to make economic use of the general cover, without compromising on visibility. Cheats can be in the form of fewer angles for general cover, fewer general colour washes, colour washes from fewer angles, variegated colour washes, and the use of devices such as colour changers and remote gobo changers. A typical repertory venue will establish a good all-purpose general cover that is rarely changed, allowing the designers to concentrate their efforts on show-specific design work.

General cover is naturally greedy for a variety of reasons; not least because many theatre-in-the-round venues are small and therefore have a very short throw from grid to floor. Short throw requires more luminaires per square foot of stage than a longer throw simply to get a decent wash at head height. More obviously, each stage area needs to be lit with twice as many instruments as the McCandless rule allows, thus doubling the size of the rig to produce the same result.

Figure 2 also shows that a theatre-in-the-round does not necessarily have a round stage, but refers to the fact that the seating is arranged all around the performance space. For this reason theatre-in-the-round is also known as 'arena stage', particularly in the Americas.

Taking into consideration the available throw from grid height, the first decision is how many stage areas are required to get a good, even general cover. The number of stage areas is also partially dependent upon the shape of the stage, although it should ideally be an odd number to allow

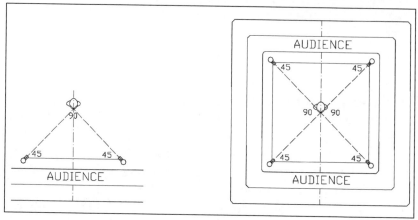

Figure 2: Applying the 90° rule to theatre-in-the-round.

for the centre area to be independently lit whenever required. Once the main acting area is covered, the entrances should also be considered, as they are surprisingly important in this staging format.

The square stages at Stephen Joseph Theatre (Westwood), The Old Laundry Theatre in Bowness, and the Royal National Theatre Cottesloe (theatre-in-the-round format) all work reasonably well with nine stage areas forming a simple ring with a centre area.

To establish the required number of stage areas draw a section (or two sections if the stage shape is not symmetrical) to calculate the number and type of luminaires required to build up a general cover from one side of the stage to the other. Be certain to check the integrity of the wash at head height by using 'stick-man' elevations, or by marking a horizontal line at head height on the section. If there is an established pool of equipment in the venue, the beam angles and therefore quantity of luminaires required to cross the stage will be dictated by the available equipment (see *Figure 17* in the chapter **Nightmares From Round Street** for an example of a sectional drawing). If it is possible to specify the

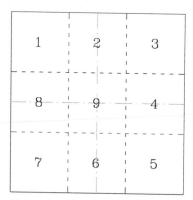

Figure 3: A nine area square stage.

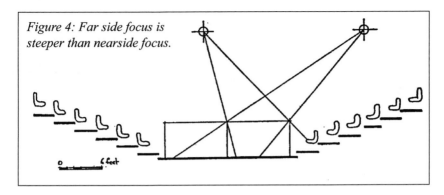

Figure 4: Far side focus is steeper than nearside focus.

equipment for the venue, there are more options open in deciding upon the number of stage areas to be used. Scarborough Westwood general cover consisted almost entirely of 500W Fresnels, but I have also worked in venues where assorted profiles or Parcans made up the general cover.

If the set design includes any sort of flying piece, it is essential to examine sections from all angles. Even a small pendant light fitting can do endless damage in terms of casting shadows, and each shadow is multiplied by four (or three in the case of the 120° rule) so the general cover may have to be adapted to compensate for these problems. This compromise may be a matter of filling in shadows with extra luminaires, or just moving some of the spotlights a few inches from their normal positions.

Take great care with focusing to the far side of the stage; the angle here will naturally be steeper than the leading edge of the stage to help keep spill out of the auditorium. However, if the focus is too tight an actor will not be lit when standing at the edge of the stage – which is invariably where the director places him for his most important speeches. This is demonstrated in greater depth in the chapter **Nightmares from Round Street** *Figure 18.*

Note that in *Figure 4* the cut-off point for focusing allows some light to spill into the auditorium. Of course it is far neater to avoid this happening altogether, but you will certainly find that the actors are much darker at the edge of the stage than in the centre if you try such a method. This diagram (of Stephen Joseph's) demonstrates a particularly difficult staging format for the lighting designer, because the stage is raised above the height of the front row. When the front row is higher than the stage, the job becomes much easier and can be visualised in this diagram by assuming the rectangular area to be actor head-height rather than stage height.

This diagram also demonstrates a good focus cut-off point. To give taller actors a better chance, the focus can be lifted to the top of the seat backs, but remember for children's shows to trim the focus even tighter than shown in this diagram. A five-year-old in the front row is much shorter than his parents, and young eyes are more susceptible to damage from direct light sources, so dazzling the children is really unacceptable both aesthetically and in terms of their own safety and comfort.

A square-shaped stage is probably the easiest shape to divide up and work with, and many stages will work with just nine stage areas plus vom[8] coverage, as demonstrated in *Figure 3*.

If each of the nine stage areas is to be lit from all four sides or corners, as a simple adaptation of the McCandless 45° rule into an 'in-the-round 90° rule' would dictate, a minimum of 36 instruments is required just to illuminate

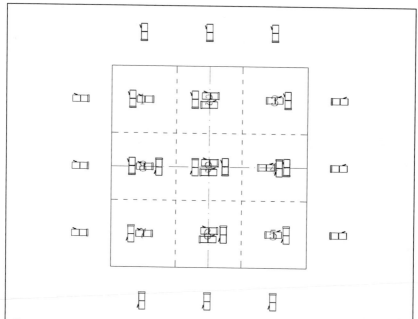

Figure 5: Nine areas each lit from four sides. One colour wash only, no specials or vom coverage.

---

[8] Vom: Short for 'vomitory', Latin for actors' entrance through a tunnel.

a relatively small stage in one colour only. Multiply this quantity with each desired colour wash and add at least two more luminaires per colour, per entrance. For a two-colour wash and four entrances lit with two instruments each, the total equipment count is already up to 88 luminaires just for basic general cover. In a budget conscious regional theatre, this does not leave much scope for specials.

This simple calculation demonstrates that even a good stock of equipment gets used up quickly just by washing the stage with light, without even thinking about any specials. This is the first of Stephen Joseph's rules to be broken, as he stated:

> *"Allow about six extra spotlights for each play in repertoire, up to a maximum of 30. The total number of spotlights has now reached 60."*

… and you will certainly want to use more than six specials per show!

Congratulations! By creating a smooth general cover, the first lighting theatre-in-the-round nightmare has also been created. Notice how a gaggle of equipment naturally congregates in groups in prime areas of the grid such as the centre. And the example in *Figure 5* shows only one colour wash and no vom lighting. In the diagram the example shows lighting directions from all four sides. Lighting from the four corners may be preferable depending upon the layout of the seating and the bars. But either way, if you add cross-washes to the general rig at a 45° or 60° angle you have the same flexibility of mixing between the two.

Using Stephen Joseph's 120° rule rather than lighting from all four sides helps to alleviate this problem, and if two-colour washes are required, they can be given a 60° offset to prevent further grid congestion.

Lighting a stage from three sides rather than four can be very 'cost effective' in terms of using fewer instruments for general cover, and therefore allows more spotlights to be used as specials. The basic principles are just the same because the stage must be divided into 'lightable' areas and sections need to be used to calculate the number of areas and instruments required, but only three luminaires are used in each stage area instead of four. At first it doesn't sound like much of a saving, but if there are nine areas and two colour washes, that's a saving of 18 instruments which are then available for use as specials. The more stage areas that are required for the general cover, the greater the savings made by using the 120° rule.

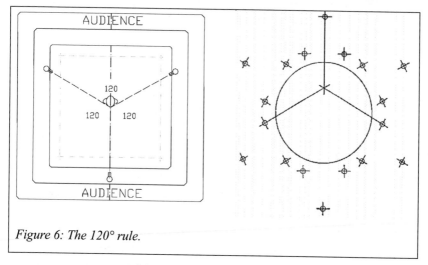

Figure 6: The 120° rule.

An alternative possibility to the fervour of lighting from four sides but the compromise of three, is to have a 'main general cover' using the 90° rule and a second (less important) colour wash rigged by the 120° rule. This provides some instrument (and circuit) saving over a conventional two-colour wash, but also ensures that the general cover is very smooth from all sides. When both washes are used in balance with each other, the result is a seven-sided wash virtually guaranteed to be free of dark spots.

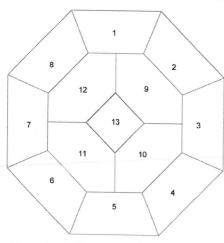

Figure 7: A thirteen area hexagonal stage.

The more elaborate the stage shape, the more (and smaller stage areas are required. *Figure 3* demonstrated a square stage divided into nine acting areas and *Figure 7* demonstrates a hexagonal stage divided into 13 areas (this is based upon Rose Bruford College's Rose Theatre).

The general cover in this venue was designed as a slight compromise between three and four-sided covers. It started as three-sided cover, but the available rigging angles were

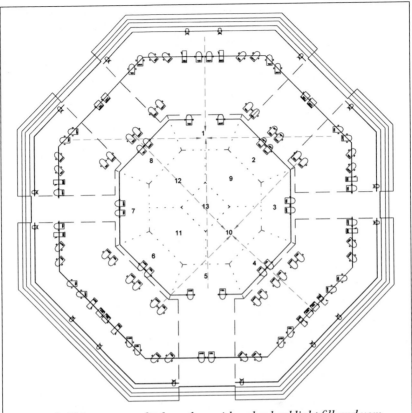

Figure 8: Thirteen areas lit from three sides plus backlight fill and vom coverage.

not symmetrical enough to produce smooth cover, so some backlight fill was added to supplement the three-sided method resulting in an almost true four-sided cover, but with an imbalance of luminaire types used for the backlight angle.

The rig was designed around this three-four sided compromise plus vom coverage in two colours. The resulting general rig comprised of a somewhat excessive 124 instruments.

There are plenty of rules to be obeyed or broken when designing a general cover, but you will have noted how large these general rigs can become. Ultimately, the design of the general cover will depend upon how many luminaires are available and how many are required for specials – as well as the available rigging points and dimmer distribution in the grid.

In a repertoire season, I would strongly recommend the use of a 'near permanent' general cover that will be used as general acting area lighting for all the shows in the season. Of course, colours can be changed between the shows, and sometimes the focus of some of these general instruments will have to be tweaked to allow for flying pieces or other staging oddities, but leaving the general rig alone as much as possible will help to cut down on the work-load of turnarounds. This time consideration is particularly important in venues where the only access to the grid is from ladders, as the turn-around time must be shared between lighting, set, and stage management. From personal experience, some of the reasons I have had to deviate from a standard general cover throughout a whole season have been to:

- Accommodate flying pieces
- Work with a set using revolves that effectively changed the shape of the main acting area (see *Figure 11*)
- To cover odd-shaped sets (see *Figure 15*)

Two Cover, or Not Two Cover ...

The solution to this question is partially answered by how you would normally work if the production were to be presented in a proscenium theatre. Does the show require two or more colour washes, or is one wash plus specials adequate?

Across seven years at the Stephen Joseph Theatre, I only used a true two colour wash once (one at 90°, one at 120°), but often managed to cheat the rig so that it appeared to have more than one colour wash.

It is easy to define 'general cover', and it is easy to define 'specials'.

However, my 'pseudo-two colour' rigs comprised a general rig plus specials, plus what I came to call 'cross-wash'.

The cross-wash was in addition to the general cover, but only lit the acting area from one side. A rig might contain two or three of these 'cross-washes' that would be used on top of general cover to add some stronger colours, or in contrast with each other. This results in an interesting and versatile rig, and manages to break a couple more of Stephen Joseph's basic rules: the use of colour, and the use of single-sided illumination.

"It is not usual to fit colour filters to spotlights to the extent that

is common practice for proscenium stage work . . . of course colour may be used ... but the main scheme will not depend upon it."

Using one or two contrasting coloured cross-washes provides great potential for actor modelling, which can be lacking when a single colour general rig is used. The coloured cross-washes add depth and atmosphere to the general lighting.

"Single [sided] spotlights are seldom used ..."

Using a strong single sided keylight also helps with actor and settings modelling, as well as other lighting essentials such as time of day and location. The most interesting plays for lighting in-the-round are those that are set outdoors over a duration of 12 or 24 hours. To achieve the right effect, the direction of keylight must be constantly changing throughout the show, which not only tells the time, but is also essential from the audience point of view. It is possible to create some very theatrical, dramatic, or even beautiful stage pictures with lighting in theatre-in-the-round, but this is useless if only a quarter of the audience get to see it for two hours. I always tried to change the direction of the keylight in each scene, both for the benefit of the audience, and as a design challenge!

Once you start designing with cross-washes, the line between 'general' and 'special' starts to become rather blurred, but you will find that being able to balance between the two makes a basic rig more versatile and visually more interesting.

Kath Geraghty (Senior Technician, Stephen Joseph Theatre) on the other hand favours using a two colour general cover. Not two completely separate washes, but a warm and cool colour in alternate instruments in the general cover. This method provides built-in modelling qualities to the light as every audience member always sees two colours on the performers. This method is very flattering to the actors, but only works well when there are enough dimmers to individually circuit every luminaire in the cover so that the lighting designer has total control of the balance between the two colours.

What is Backlight Anyway?

It is fair to argue that there is no such as thing as backlight in theatre-in-the-round because every backlight is someone else's front light. However, the opposite can also be argued because an actor can only face in one direction at any time so he therefore always has a light behind him, which by definition is his backlight. Of course there are exceptions to this like all rules. A strong keylight from behind an actor can have great dramatic effect, just as it can in a proscenium; but for general illumination, how can it be made clear in notes sessions what exactly any individual is referring to when using the expressions front or backlight?

It never occurred to me that this was an interesting question because it was something that always resolved itself subconsciously at Scarborough. Perhaps that was the benefit of working in a small team, mainly with only one or two directors. You get to understand each others' meanings on a deeper level than words alone allow. However when I spent the first season of The Rose Theatre working with Rose Bruford College lighting students this perception of front and back light did become an issue. With hindsight maybe I should have explained it with more clarity, but for me it was a natural assumption.

The whole season was interesting (and fun) because it was the first time the theatre was put to use, and work was being done around contractors trying to finish the job. When the students were finally allowed into the theatre, there was plenty of experimenting to be done in terms of which bars to rig parts of the general cover on, how to balance the Parcans against the Minuettes in some of the acting areas, what colours to use in the general wash, and so on.

Some of the students were understandably a little nervous at being the 'guinea-pigs' in the new theatre for their degree projects, and as lighting designers they were asking my advice on some of their lighting scenes. I have to say that they did remarkably well considering some of the 'circumstances beyond our control' that were causing scheduling problems, but the reason for this anecdotal story is in order to define 'backlight'.

Figure 8 shows the Rose general cover. Most of it – the three-sided cover – was created with Parcans. The additional fourth side fill was by Fresnels, and for the eight outer stage areas, Minuettes were used due to their proximity both to the acting areas and to the audience. Unfortunately, they were quite difficult to focus because the angle was very flat. However, there were no other rigging points to enable the outer edges of the stage to be lit, so the lighting designers (as is often the way) had to 'go with the flow'!

During notes sessions, I found that I was frequently suggesting that the front and backlight balance needed adjusting. The backlight was often too strong in relation to the front light.

When I returned for the rehearsal after the notes session, I found that the balance was even worse – contrary to my suggestion, instead of reducing the strength of the backlight, the students had increased it.

Then I realised what had happened ... I worked with a few of the students and asked them to stand in one of the outer eight stage areas, and point to its frontlight. They all pointed at a Minuette – the backlight! They must have though I was mad when I suggested the rebalance if we were referring to the opposite luminaires as front and backlight!

Afterwards the reason for the confusion was obvious. In a proscenium theatre, the frontlight comes from behind the audience. The Minuettes were rigged behind the audience so it was therefore logical that they were the frontlight for those stage areas.

However in theatre-in-the-round the opposite is true, because if an actor is at the edge of the stage, he will almost always be facing into the centre of the stage where he can address the majority of the audience. Hence the light coming from behind him and his audience block is his backlight.

For this reason, directors will inevitably position actors towards the edges of the stage, or even in the vom mouths for important speeches.

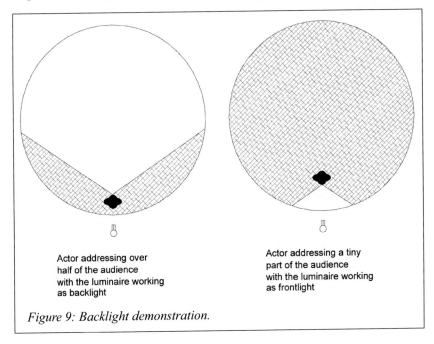

Actor addressing over
half of the audience
with the luminaire working
as backlight

Actor addressing a tiny
part of the audience
with the luminaire working
as frontlight

Figure 9: Backlight demonstration.

Photograph 7: 'Love Off The Shelf', Lighting: Jackie Staines,
Set: Jan Bee Brown, Photograph: Jackie Staines

Figure 9 demonstrates how the actor can encompass far more members of the audience from these positions, and if the stage is square and the actor is in a vom mouth, he can address 90% of the audience without turning his head.

For the director, the vom mouth is one of the most important stage areas. For the lighting designer it is one of the most difficult, because the light must be somehow contained within the vom walls without spilling sideways into the audience. When I first started working at the Stephen Joseph Theatre, Pattern 23s were commonly used for lighting directly into the vom mouths, but the edges of the beams tended to be visible (even with a light Hamburg frost) when the actors moved through them. Wherever possible, I started using PCs for this job instead, so as to soften the edge further, but to keep to the vom wall containment.

The photograph (7) of Sara Markland in *Love Off The Shelf* shows the use of contrasting vom front and backlight, although in this instance the frontlight was by ADB 1kW Fresnel + colour wheel, and the backlight by Silhouette 30 + colour wheel and light Hamburg Frost.

Using Sections and Elevations

Sectional drawings will help the designer foresee any potential problems when devising a general cover standard rig. When this general cover is working well and the beam angles are familiar to the designer, adding cross-washes and most specials is relatively easy providing that there are no obstacles in the way.

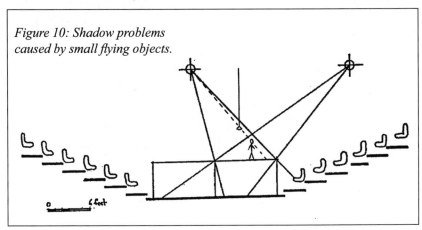

Figure 10: Shadow problems caused by small flying objects.

As soon as any solid object is flown from the grid the use of sectional drawings becomes essential and also if the stage height varies it is advisable to work with elevations to ensure that both the general cover and the specials will work at the higher level.

Even the smallest of objects can cause big problems: a simple pendant light fitting is a potential shadow causing problem, and the shadow of course is multiplied three or four times for each colour wash.

Figure 10, which is an adaptation of the section shown in *Figure 4*, demonstrates a single light fitting causing a shadow through most of the useful part of the light beam of one side of a general wash area. However, light fittings are relatively easy to cope with because there is a good chance that the offending instruments can be simply shuffled a few inches along the bar until they no longer cast a shadow of the cable.

This 'avoidance tactic' is satisfactory for one or two fittings, but if there are several such fittings in the set design, and the rig contains many specials, grid space quickly becomes an issue.

Photograph 8: 'Rocket To The Moon', Lighting: Jackie Staines,
Set: Juliet Nichols, Photograph: Adrian Gatie

---

[9] Stephen Joseph Theatre

Photograph 9: 'Dreams From A Summerhouse', Lighting: Jackie Staines,
Set: Juliet Nichols, Photograph: Adrian Gatie

Curiously, it is often the small items like light fittings that can cause the worst problems. Larger items have to be worked around more thoroughly, so the results are less of a compromise. Occasionally, the flying pieces might even provide an unusual or useful opportunity to deliberately cast shadows. A couple of examples of this at SJT[9] (Westwood) are *Rocket To The Moon* and *Dreams From a Summerhouse*.

Rocket to The Moon contained both problematic and opportunistic flying pieces. The problems were caused by five pendant light fittings that affected about three-quarters of the general cover. The 'opportunity' was created by a large overhead fan in the centre of the stage, which was an integral part of both the action and the dialogue. Part of the director's brief was to create a heady, oppressive atmosphere. By lighting directly through the fan when it was turning slowly, the resulting moving shadow became as much a part of the action as the fan itself, along with its accompanying 'whooshing' sound effect.

Dreams From a Summerhouse provided a more unusual lighting opportunity in that a mixture of real and artificial foliage was suspended from the whole of the lighting grid! The show was set outside in a garden, and the set was very realistic with real grass and trees – which for some reason became my job to keep alive during the run. The branches and leaves were hung below the luminaires, which meant that focusing through the branches was both difficult and painful, but it created the best ever 'gobo wash', and saved my budget because I didn't have to buy any. The lighting was textured, atmospheric and realistic – once it was eventually focused!

Using Colour in the General Cover
As Stephen Joseph said:

> *"It is not usual to fit colour filters to spotlights to the extent that is common practice for proscenium stage work ... of course colour may be used ... but the main scheme will not depend upon it."*

A general cover would be expected to be either open white, or in very neutral tones, and if two covers are used, in a classic cool and warm (steel and straw) format.

Some stage lighting textbooks have also shown a single wash using contrasting warms and cools on opposite sides. In this book I do not intend to generalise about the use of colour in the main basic cover as I preferred to select all of my colours on a show-by-show basis, although I have witnessed entire seasons where the colour of the general cover was never changed. However, what follows are some examples of how on occasions I deviated a long way from what could be described as the 'norm' for colouring general cover.

For the majority of shows I did indeed use neutral colours:

Supergel #09	Gold	
Lee 202	Daylight Correction	
Supergel #54	Pale Lilac	

However, on a few occasions I went as dark as Supergel #68 (sky blue) or even #74 (night blue)!

I used Supergel #68 throughout the general rig of *Dreams From A Summerhouse* because of its quality to blend as a 24 hour colour. Depending upon the other colours in use at the time, #68 can give the impression of night or day, and is particularly useful for scenes set at dusk. This show is discussed in greater detail in the chapter **Painting The Stage**.

In *Gaslight*, I used a different sort of 'cheat' in colouring the general rig. I created a similar effect to using a general cover plus cross-washes, but saved on the quantity of luminaires by not actually rigging any cross-

Photograph 10: 'Gaslight', Lighting: Jackie Staines,
Set: Jan Bee Brown, Photograph: Adrian Gatie

washes at all. In this example, the main source of illumination was to be keyed from the centre of the stage outwards. This meant that the outer ring of general cover luminaires would naturally need to be plotted at lower levels than the others, but due to pairing restrictions (only 60 dimmers at SJT Westwood), this was not possible. The solution was to use a 'variegated' general wash, where the colours were different throughout the whole rig. Paler colours were used in the centre near to the practical light fitting and source of keylight, and these faded into darker colours towards the perimeter of the rig giving the impression of the light fading away at the edges. In one corner of the rig, the colours from the outer sides of the general cover were in complete contrast to the rest of the general cover as they were in an area keyed from a fireplace. The resulting general cover was made from the following colours:

Lee 138	Pale green
Lee 147	Apricot
Lee 242	Fluorescent 4300°K
Supergel #68	Sky Blue
Supergel #74	Night Blue

… and the results of this blended mix of colours could be clearly seen as reflection on the high-gloss black floor!

It was an interesting exercise both in creating atmosphere and in a slightly unusual use of colour. When people ask me what I think was my best design at Scarborough it is not a question that can be easily answered because different shows are good or bad for different reasons, but this production of *Gaslight* (superbly directed by Malcolm Hebden) always features in my mental list of proud achievements. For that reason, I am pleased to include Michael Northen's *Focus* review of *Gaslight* in this book because he voices some of his old proscenium fears over theatre-in-the-round:

Taking his own regional initiative, Association of Lighting Designers (ALD) Chairman Michael Northen visited our Regional Organiser Jackie Staines on her home turf in Scarborough.

I was extremely flattered to be invited by Jackie Staines to Scarborough to see a production of 'Gaslight' which she had lit. Having willingly accepted I hadn't taken into account two important factors. Firstly that the train journey from Cheltenham to Scarborough takes or should take four-and-a-half hours. Mine took an extra hour as it happened to be the hottest day of the year (93 degrees). Outside Derby we came to a grinding halt as we were told that the railway lines had buckled. Secondly I remembered that the play took place in the Stephen Joseph Theatre in the Round, a type of theatre that I am not over keen on and wondered how on earth they could get away with producing a play that was originally written for a prosc. theatre. This thought of it intrigued me immensely.

My hour late arrival at the theatre was greeted by an anxious expression on Jackie's face, who feared that I had either forgotten to turn up or decided not to come. The theatre was a hive of activity. Although it was lunch time, people seemed to be flying in and out of doors, rostra being covered in the passage outside the box office, and little huddles of earnest groups in deep conversation. The atmosphere was so hectic that I didn't dare suggest a drink, but said that it would be great just to see the inside of the auditorium if there was time. Jackie readily agreed.

Once inside under the stark working lights the glamourous image of a theatre seemed to evaporate. Stark it certainly was. The square acting area surrounded by tiered seats looked very small, and very unexciting. The furniture and props on the stage were the only indication that a period play was to be performed that evening. As there were no walls surrounding the acting area on which to hang pictures and all the paraphernalia that goes to make up a Victorian room I wondered how the gas brackets which play such an important part could have been disregarded. Being a clever and inventive lot they had substituted in place of the wall brackets a neat Victorian chandelier suspended over the table centre stage.

The reason for my visit was to see Jackie at work and the production of 'Gaslight'; a play which I had worked on many times though never in the round. I soon realised that I was talking to a lighting designer totally dedicated to theatre in the round, and I listened intently to all her arguments without daring to interrupt. I thought it wise to leave any comments until after seeing the show. She explained in detail the working of her layout and how she had to cope with three entirely different plays in the repertoire with little time available for resetting or refocusing. She pointed out the multitude of assorted lamps hanging from a grid suspended from the ceiling above the acting area, and how it was necessary to have about fifty percent of the rig permanently focused on the acting area allowing the rest of the lamps to be moved about and used where they were needed for any other productions. It was nice to see that the old faithful Patt. 123 was still in use. I was also wily enough to notice the crafty coloured tapes on the bars indicating the position of lamps for each play. Not only did she have to worry about the main house productions but also the small studio theatre which seemed to be in constant use. The next port of call was the operating box positioned behind the last row of seats, with a good view of the stage, which accommodated the stage manager, and the lighting and sound operators. I asked Jackie what happened if anyone dried, with the stage manager cum prompter seated behind a sheet of glass, without any communication with the stage other than through a microphone. The alarming answer came that it was just too bad and that they would have to rely on their fellow actors to feed the necessary lines.

I could see that Jackie was keen to return to her work so quietly I said I would retire to my hotel and return in time for the show. The hotel found by Jackie was very comfortable overlooking the sea, but nothing in Scarborough seemed to be on the flat. I found an excellent Chinese restaurant and returned to the theatre in plenty of time for the show. I sat down in the bar with a large drink in one hand and the most informative programme in the other, both of which I thoroughly enjoyed. But my great joy and surprise was moving into the theatre and seeing the previously stark and uninviting auditorium transformed due entirely to the introduction of Jackie's preset lighting. I thought she had managed a wonderful job, and spent the remainder of the time before the show started trying to find out how she had achieved it. I was very tempted to walk onto the stage - which is very easy to do in this theatre - and see what lamps were doing what. I now felt distinctly better and began to warm to the theatre in the round and couldn't wait for the play to start.

It wasn't long before I was completely immersed in the play, which had been beautifully produced by Malcolm Hebden. I so admired how he overcame the difficult problem of playing a long scene without having his actors with their backs to any part of the theatre for any length of time. Although this necessitated considerable restlessness on the part of the actors, one soon became used to it and took it for granted. However it was not long before my eyes wondered back naturally to Jackie's lighting. What I always enjoy in any production is the use of strong contrasting colours. Jackie certainly wasn't afraid of choosing her colours, creating the heavy atmosphere which the play demands using deep dark blues contrasting with a strong yellow range. The fading of the gas chandelier was very effective especially with the accompanying wheeze, which I don't think was Jackie's responsibility. The splendid cast went through the play without a hitch and I didn't detect a single dry. I only had one slight niggle which was about the white table cloth used later in the play. Naturally Jackie had concentrated quite a battery of lights on the table centre stage. All was well until the white table cloth was laid. Then one could look at nothing else. I was always brought up in the dim and distant past to dye anything white in a bucket of weak tea, which will always get you out of that sort of trouble.

The play was over far too soon, and I met Jackie for a drink in the bar. We had a long discussion on the pros and cons of theatre in the round, and I could see I was not getting anywhere with my arguments in favour of the proscenium stage. She was absolutely adamant that there was only one way to produce a play and that was in the round and she was going to stick to it.

Looking around it was all too obvious that the theatre was very pushed for space. I was so pleased to be shown the plans for the future theatre which looks most exciting. The huge ex-Odeon cinema has been bought and is in the middle of being converted. Having seen the set up I must be truthful and say I was very impressed with the theatre and all the hard work Jackie puts into her side of it.

3 HOW SPECIAL ARE SPECIALS?

How Special Are Specials?

Sometimes it is hard to distinguish where the general cover ends and the specials begin. Is a special still a special if it used throughout the whole show instead of just for special effects?

I have already mentioned 'cross-washes' on several occasions, but this is a prime example of the grey area between general cover and specials. The cross-wash provides some general illumination so it could be considered as part of the general rig, but its colour and angle are specific to the show, or even the scene, so it should be considered as 'special'. The angle of the cross wash is often determined by the physical position of practicals or other obvious sources of keylight, therefore despite their nature of general illumination they are definitely specials. In a busy show, perhaps a musical or children's show, two cross washes from opposite sides rigged with colour changers can provide great potential whilst tying up relatively few luminaires.

What is Keylight in-the-round?

Part of the lighting designer's brief is to create an atmosphere appropriate to the setting. The very nature of theatre-in-the-round is that there is often little or no setting at all, so the lighting designer must create the setting itself as well as the atmosphere. This is actually advantageous because you end up with total control over directional lighting, so you can ensure that you can make maximum use of available rigging angles and change the direction of the keylight several times during the show. If you have to light a set where the (virtual) windows, doors, and light fittings are all on the same side, you have a battle on your hands to ensure a good lighting balance all through the show.

In this context, keylight is cross washes, practicals cover, sun or moonlight key and windows, which will often consist of gobos projected across the floor, and also the more obvious specials such as soliloquy spots, set highlights, and anything built into the set or the fabric of the auditorium itself. If the script refers to light fittings, it is worth liaising with the set designer early on to ensure that the fittings are placed in the most useful positions.

Strong directional light can be wonderful for modelling and creating atmospheres but it is essential to view these scenes from all sides of the auditorium during rehearsals. A strong keylight will work well when viewed from either of the sides. When viewed from the same angle as the key, or from the opposite side, the key will look less pleasing. The 'front' may well look too bright and the 'back' too dark, but with excessive modelling over the heads and shoulders. If the scene is short, strong balances like this are perfectly acceptable, but if the scene is longer – maybe the whole act – the lighting must be changed during the course of the scene to alleviate eye fatigue on the dark side. If it is not possible to change the direction of the keylight, for example by an actor turning on another light fitting, then these problems can be eased by slow and subtle follow-on cues. You can make the scene setting statement with a strong key, but follow it up with a slow build of the general wash after a few minutes. If the fade time is long enough, the audience will not notice the change at all, whereas they would notice the eye fatigue if this measure was not taken. Good team work with the set designer can prevent these types of problems from occurring in the first place.

The best opportunity for the lighting designer to vary the keylight direction is a show that has many short scenes and allows the lighting balance to change continuously throughout the performance. The formula is simple: position the key light sources in as many different places on the setting as possible. A piece located centre-stage will require light emanating outwards as described in the *Gaslight* example, and light fittings positioned at the edges of the stage or 'windows' will require a one-sided wash lighting across the width of the stage. The further this wash spreads, the more useful it becomes. Although small pools of light are often more realistic, it can become distracting if the audience are constantly aware of actors moving in and out of light.

A good example of a potential problem caused by many small keylights can be seen in photograph 11, the set for *Conversations With My Father*. The front row of seats was removed from the auditorium and replaced with pub style seating booths. Some of these booths were used by the actors, and some of them were sold to unsuspecting audience members as ordinary seats. As well as providing a lighting problem, it was a great example of the intimacy of theatre-in-the-round so keenly enthused by both Stephen

Photograph 11: 'Conversations With My Father', Lighting: Jackie Staines,
Set: Jan Bee Brown, Photograph: Adrian Gatie

Joseph and Alan Ayckbourn. The actors and the audience virtually merged
into one when the tables were being cleared and cleaned in some scenes
during this show, and the audience were never quite sure whether or not
they would be sharing their table with a performer!

There were about 10 small practical light fittings placed in between the
booths. It was natural to key from the outside edge of the stage inwards to
complement these fixtures, but the sheer quantity combined with problems
with lighting the centre area resulted in potential balancing difficulties. It
was a tricky task to get the balance across the whole stage smooth enough
without losing the pub atmosphere.

This show was one of the occasions when parts of the general rig had to be repositioned in order to compensate for a flying piece. The four Minuette Fresnels that were used to light stage area 9 – the centre – had to be moved outwards because in their original positions they focused straight through the bottle shelf structure. In their original positions (had the flying piece not been there) they would have comfortably lit an actor standing anywhere inside the central bar area. When re-rigged to avoid the bottle shelf they would only light into their own side of the bar, which was effectively useless. In order to light to the opposite side of the central bar area, the angle was terribly flat, and it was only because of the booths being part of the set rather than conventional auditorium seating that they could be used at all. If the normal audience seating had been left in situ the centre area lighting would have dazzled the front row. Although the booths allowed these instruments to be used to some extent, the angle was so displeasing and the bar area so important in the staging and content of the play that some additional and tightly focused instruments were required to provide general illumination for a standard stage area but in a rather special way.

After several meetings with the designer and the carpenter, and many elevation drawings later, between us we were able to design the bottle shelf in such a way that it invisibly accommodated eight 75W Birdies that served the purpose exceptionally well.

This staging problem was an excellent example of the importance both of adequate drawings and of sensible production meetings. This show is also an example of when something that appears to be going terribly wrong works out better for everyone concerned.

The original set design had the booths, the Wurlitzer, the flying piece and the bar, but the floor was supposed to be covered with white tiles, which were not something a lighting designer looked forward to anyway. As it turned out, they proved far too expensive for the show budget, so the set designer was also despondent at this point. The problem resolved itself after a visit to a local American restaurant that had narrow natural wood floorboards that provided the inspiration for a set redesign. A few enquires later and a source of these floorboards was discovered from salvage. The decision was made to exchange the white tiles for a natural wood floor which was both evocative of the period and setting, and very pleasing to the eye because of the way in which it seemed to absorb the colours of

Photograph 12: 'Rocket To The Moon', Lighting: Jackie Staines,
Set: Juliet Nichols, Photograph: Jackie Staines

the lighting. However, it was not so pleasing to the carpenter because it took three days and nights to lay – much of the salvaged timber was so damp that it was badly warped and didn't want to stay flat!

Sometimes a single practical light fitting itself becomes a very special special. Used on its own or with just minimal use of its accompanying cover, it can prove remarkably effective for short dramatic moments.

Photograph 12 shows Kenneth Price in the closing moments of a scene from *Rocket To The Moon*. He was lit by the reflection of the table lamp in the glass tabletop, a tiny amount of fill from the practical's cover, and some blue backlight keyed through the aforementioned ceiling fan. The intimacy of theatre-in-the-round allows plotting at very low intensities so it is possible to create subtle balances that would not be seen in a proscenium theatre.

Practicals and their associated covering luminaires can therefore be considered as either general wash or specials, depending upon their use specific to each show. Practicals in theatre-in-the-round can be quite difficult to use if no consideration of the cabling requirements has been made at the set design stage. In a proscenium production it is often quite acceptable to have the cable running visibly off stage, however this is not the case in theatre-in-the-round both aesthetically or in terms of health and safety if the audience have to walk across the set to get to their seats. Again it is worth liaising closely with the set designer and carpenter if floor level practicals are required. This also applies to other luminaires that may need to be built into the set itself, such as under-floor lighting, Birdies in discreet and strategic places, anything on trucks, etc.

If the reader ever gets the opportunity of designing a theatre-in-the-round installation, please provide adequate circuits at stage floor level. And adequate is at least twice the quantity that you first thought of!

Keylight is, in the words of Kath Geraghty (Senior Technician, Stephen Joseph Theatre):

"Fun, useful, and stops things looking bland."

But importantly, every keylight in the design must have a reason. When the reason is established, you have a reason for modelling the performers. Kath observed of Alan Ayckbourn's direction:

"He always knows where the windows are."

Even if none are referred to in the script or by the set design, Alan will brief the lighting designer on the geography of the room that the show is set in and even if there is no verbal reference, he will often put in a bit of 'looking out of the window acting', which gives the lighting designer the key motivation to base the design around.

Effects, Pyrotechnics and Smoke

It is possible to use any of the standard special effects that are used in proscenium theatres provided there are suitable routes for cables and pipes, and that all necessary safety precautions are adhered to. Some effects such as UV and dry ice can be particularly effective.

When the stage floor itself is the set, tricks with UV and invisible paint can completely transform it – much to the delight of children who having walked across the floor think that they know exactly what it looks like!

Invisible paint was used extensively on the minimalistic set for *Mr. A's Amazing Maze Plays*, so it was capable of changing from a warm and inviting playground to somewhere very mysterious once the paint began to show.

There is one obvious drawback with using ultra-violet floods and that is that they do tend to flood everywhere, but during focusing this cannot be seen. It's only when the first audience arrives wearing white or fluorescent day-glo T-shirts that you get to see the real extent of the problem!

Smoke and dry ice can both be very effective but they do have inherent difficulties. Firstly there is the question of transportation and how to get the effect to the stage. Making a small hole for a practical's cable is easy enough, but making a four inch hole for a smoke duct is another matter. Both smoke and dry ice are noisy and this can also be a consideration. Often a smoke effect has been accompanied by some sort of sound effect just in order to disguise the noise of the smoke machine itself. Once on stage, the behaviour of the smoke is determined by the air-conditioning. It is essential to organise a smoke technical rehearsal with same amount of air-conditioning as will be used during performances. Even then a carefully timed smoke cue can go wrong once there is an audience producing a new set of warm air currents.

Hopefully the smoke effect can disperse naturally, but sometimes it may be necessary to artificially remove the smoke as quickly as possible by increasing the air-conditioning. At this point the technical rehearsal becomes very tedious because it is more about air-conditioning management than lighting or effects. However, it is worth the effort because smoke and dry ice effects can only work properly if they are totally predictable.

Pyrotechnics are by far the most difficult effects to accommodate in theatre-in-the-round because of the proximity of the audience. All safety instructions issued with the effect must be adhered to, but otherwise, if there is somewhere to run the cable and install the pod – use them if required. Once again though, the technical rehearsal must be using realistic air conditioning to establish the effect of a large smoke burst, and then extracting that smoke.

One of the best special effects at Westwood was in *Neville's Island* when the cast had to cook sausages on stage on a camping stove. Firstly the stove had to be rigged by the cast and pick up power from somewhere (buried in the stage floor), but the look, sound, and smell of frying sausages on stage – complete with a fatty smoke plume – sent the audience running to the snack bar in the interval!

4 PAINTING THE STAGE

Painting the Stage

As well as the essential task of lighting the performers, the lighting designer working in proscenium has the opportunity of lighting the scenery both for illumination and for atmosphere. The very nature of theatre-in-the-round is to use furniture rather than conventional scenery in straight plays, or even no scenery at all, and to create the settings just with lighting, sound, and props. In many ways these types of shows are by far the best fun for the lighting designer, as you have a free reign with the lighting and do not have to conform to any predetermined conventions presented by the set design. In this case, the stage floor becomes a canvas for the lighting designer and can be used in many ways. However, there are two points to be aware of. A gloss finished floor can be disastrous for gobo projection, and the lighting designer must be aware of what is happening at head-height. I can use the same show as an example for both of these problems. *The Village Fete* had probably the most unusual of director's briefs for me: "to create the set with light by making full size groundplans."

This brief was certainly unusual and full of inherent problems. The groundplans themselves were easy enough; simply a matter of lots of profiles with shutters and gobos projected onto the floor. The problems came when the actors walked on stage and through all these hard edges. It was obvious from the outset that there would be problems at head-height if everything were focused at floor level - which it had to be to get the pictures to work. Even if the pictures worked focused at head-height, there would still be problems with sharp beam edges.

A convention had to be established from the very beginning of the show to explain the concept of the light-set and to allow the audience to accept the minimalistic settings: just a few simple blocks for tables and chairs. As each scene began, the floor was dressed with the appropriate 'ground plan' for the scene. An actor would mime a door opening action that would be accompanied by a sound effect and a lighting change indicating light streaming through the door.

This would be followed by a slow build of the general acting area

Photograph 14: 'The Village Fete', Lighting: Jackie Staines, Set: Juliet Nichols, Photograph: Jackie Staines

lighting to illuminate the actors instead of just the floor. The convention worked well because of the actor/lighting/sound synchronisation, but also because each 'virtual' room in the house had its own distinct personality. Establishing a simple set of colours and windows for each room allowed the audience to easily identify the location each time it was re-used. Some of the colours were quite strong, but this was only to assist the audience with recognition. They were naturally washed out when the general lighting was added, and this was one of the few examples when I used an open white general cover.

The Village Fete had little in the way of set apart from a grey-dappled floor and matching block-style chairs and tables: all of which were set and removed by the actors as part of the action. The stage floor was in neutral tones to allow the gobo projection to be clearly seen, and to allow the colours to be determined purely by light. Focusing was a chore and didn't work as well as one would have hoped, because it was difficult to get enough wide angled profiles to draw the ground plans with minimal shuttering considering the 14 foot[10] grid height throw. It was a relief when the focus was finished and the first part of the technical rehearsal completed with a degree of success.

---

[10] 4.3 metre

During the night after the first half of the technical rehearsal, the floor was given a coat of varnish but unfortunately gloss instead of matt had been applied. When the technical rehearsal resumed the following day, none of the gobo projection could be seen due to the flare caused by the gloss varnish. Flare is always a bit of a problem anyway, particularly when seen from the opposite side of the auditorium to the source of the projection, but this gloss floor took it away from all angles, so the whole concept of the show was blown apart. The floor was re-coated with matt varnish the following night!

Lighting for Fun

When the focus and floor were eventually sorted out, The Village Fete was one example of how lighting theatre-in-the-round can be simply a matter of good fun for the lighting designer. The shows that delighted me the most as a designer were all of a similar format: little or no set, stylised, often children's shows or musicals. The formula was that light, sound and props created the settings, and that the floor became a canvas for painting light upon. All of these shows involved an excessive quantity of gobos, which, if you make them yourself, constitutes 'fun'.

Gobos are such a simple way of saying 'This is a room' or 'This is a forest' that they become the ideal trick for quickly setting a scene, particularly for shows aimed at a younger audience. Post-show platforms taught me that children are fascinated by these ideas and they would often ask more questions about technical theatre than they would about the performers, much to the chagrin of the actors!

Stylised shows also provide the opportunity to use bolder colours than you might have been told are 'normal' for theatre-in-the-round. One bright and funny song and out comes the Broadway Pink! A show that sticks strongly in my mind is Love Off The Shelf – a spoof musical based around two Mills & Boon authors. It was one of those shows that presented a script of questionable quality, but was turned into a real smash hit show under the superb direction of Alan Ayckbourn and the input from the cast and technical team alike.

The set was a plain floor not dissimilar to The Village Fete, but with a double revolve. There was one permanent piece of set which was a large desk in the middle of the revolve. Other set pieces were really giant props such as the grassy bank shown in photograph 7. Because of the shape of

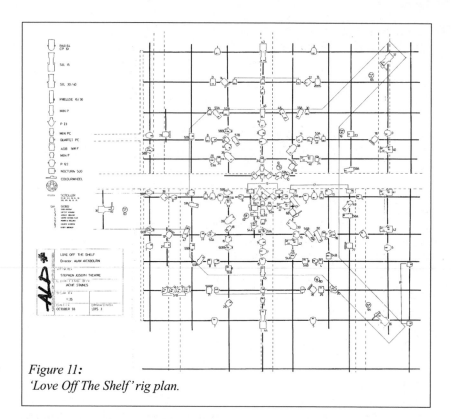

Figure 11:
'Love Off The Shelf' rig plan.

the revolve, this show was one of the occasions when I re-rigged parts of the general cover in order to complement the round shape. The outer revolve was also covered by a ring of Fresnels with scrollers fitted. Ideally there would have been 16 for this job, but the budget dictated only eight. The rig consisted of a modified general cover, extra cover plus scroller colour wash, loads of specials and tons of gobos.

The general cover was modified in terms of rigging positions in order to work with the shape of the revolve. The areas outside of the revolve, which were basically the corners of the stage plus very narrow corridors, can be seen on the plan as the Pattern 123s and Minuettes in Lee 201 (daylight correction). The rest of the general cover was focused into the revolve area and re-rigged where necessary to better follow the shape. These sub-kiloWatt Fresnels were coloured with Supergel #52 (light lavender) and supplemented with a ring of eight 1kW Fresnels in the same colour. Had the budget allowed, these 1ks would also have been fitted with scrollers. The plan therefore shows two rings of 1kW Fresnels – one with scrollers, one without – focused in opposite pairs. The lavender was chosen to blend well with all the colours in the scrollers.

The four Parcans were used at the end of the show for the big wedding finale, the bright colours (Supergel #49 medium purple, Supergel #21 golden amber, Supergel #14 medium straw and Supergel #32 medium salmon pink) reflected on the glittery alter (a clever transformation of the desk), and also lit up the dry ice from a different angle to the low level Birdies cutting through it; which is also described in the chapter *Nightmares From Round Street.*

The numerous profiles shown on the drawing were either gobos, high-lighting specific pieces of set, or were individual spotlights for solo vocalists. Notice the four Pattern 23s in the bottom left hand corner of the plan; they were a stained-glass window composite gobo which unfortunately was rigged directly underneath a structural beam. These beams were the source of many lighting problems at Westwood, and are discussed in the chapter *Nightmares From Round Street.*

Ideally a lighting designer shouldn't have to worry about peculiarities of venues in this way, but if you don't take them on board at design time, you can run into problems later and lose valuable time if equipment has to be re-rigged during the focusing session because you overlooked an obstacle. In the section *Gobo Washes Galore*, I mention the method of over-rigging some of the lanterns used in composite gobos. This technique could not be used where the smaller beams were located in the ceiling so I made sure that the beams were always the first things to be pencilled onto my drawings. They also provided useful reference points for the rigging crew and can be clearly seen in *Figure 14.*

Before reducing my ideas to eight scrollers from 16, I had toyed with the idea of using Vari*Lite VL5s to provide not only an infinite choice of colours, but also the possibility of following some of the movement around the revolve. Taking the cost implication out of the equation for a moment, trying to decide how many and where to rig the Vari*Lites was surprisingly difficult. Not from the colour point of view, hence using scrollers, but because of the movement. It was rather like trying to use followspots; by the time you've limited the movement to prevent spillage

Photograph 15: 'Love Off The Shelf', Lighting: Jackie Staines
Set: Jan Bee Brown, Photograph: Jackie Staines

into the audience, the available range of movement becomes so limited that it's hardly worth using at all. Also, to get the best effect, I would have needed so many of them to do a decent job that there would never have been enough grid space and weight and power would also have become an issue. Even if Vari*Lite had been kind enough to lend half a dozen VL5s and a control desk, I would not have been able to use them effectively.

The scenes in this show were set in the authors' office, alternating with fantasy scenes from their books. Because much of this show is fantasy, I was able to use all manner of colours and silly gobos – the production was meant to be high kitsch anyway!

Some notable examples of lighting for fun included: Birdies built into the desk behind gauze panels which were used to light a polystyrene 'cliff face' and to push light through the covering of dry ice in the finale; a carefully crafted United Nations logo gobo for the number *Lovers of the World Unite*, and an extensive use of the colour purple! This show was a great example of light, sound, set, costumes and props working in perfect harmony to create a wonderful fantasy of pure good fun.

Lighting for Darkness

It is often said that shadows are as important as lighting. There is some opinion that this is a rather pretentious statement, however there is some truth in the idea. One of the lighting designers most difficult tasks is to create an atmosphere of darkness without it being too dark. In this case it does not matter what staging format is used, it is the same problem, and a problem that will arise many times during a lighting designer's career. With a couple of show examples in mind, I have concluded that creating dark and/or atmospheric scenes in theatre-in-the-round is actually easier than in proscenium situation. The reason for this conclusion is quite simple. In theatre-in-the-round there are more available angles for contrasting cross washes and creating contrast is one of the best ways of giving the impression of darkness.

I have lit or seen many shows that are set in darkness or have dark scenes within them, and I will use several examples: *Dreams From a Summerhouse, The End Of The Food Chain, Neville's Island, Othello* and *Macbeth*.

I will begin with *Dreams From A Summerhouse* because it has already featured earlier in this book. It is a musical based on the Beauty and the

Beast story and is unusual as a production because the set is made entirely of natural materials (trees, branches, leaves, grass: see *photograph 9*), and the time span is all night long.

The script stipulated that during act one it must be very dark, but that the moon soon rises. Act two continued through the night so I was faced with the problem of maintaining a prolonged period of darkness without causing discomfort to the audience. Firstly I cheated by extending the time period from sunset to sunrise, and secondly I made good use of on-stage practicals allowing for 'cross washes' from many different angles and in surprisingly contrasting colours. Nonetheless, the overall atmosphere still had to be one of 'outdoor night' which raises the age old question of 'what colour is night?'

The question of course is really nonsense – there is no colour. Moonlight is extremely directional and therefore shadowy, but moonlight is merely reflected sunlight so the answer is that night is the same 'colour' as day, only darker. (This theory was formulated after walking the length of Scarborough sea front during a full moon!) However, the average audience readily accepts the use of dark blue lighting as a suggestion of night but there is a technical reason as well as a psychological one for using deep blues. At night, or in other dark situations, the human eye switches from colour to monochrome vision. Using a dark colour helps to kill other pigments and to force black and white vision. So deep blues were used for this purpose. The actual colours used were chosen for two good reasons. Supergel #68 is particularly good for dusk and blends well into night or day, so it was ideal for a time span of dusk 'til dawn, and Supergel #74 was used as the deep blue. There were many possible choices from the swatchbook but #74 happened to react very well with the material of Belle's dress (Belle being the beauty). Yes, I actually took a fabric sample to the electrics office to experiment with the effect of colour on it!

On top of this, there were four basic cross washes plus specials. Roughly speaking, the four washes were keyed from the four corners of the rig in different colours for different purposes, and this resulted in a remarkably symmetrical looking rig plan due to the diagonal repetition of the cross-washes.

Corner one was the moonlight key, predominantly Lee 161 (slate blue) cutting through the darker blues. Corner two was Supergel #21

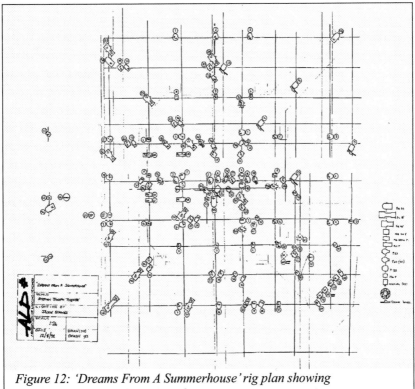

Figure 12: 'Dreams From A Summerhouse' rig plan showing symmetrical diagonal cross-washes.

(golden amber) for a late sunset feel, although this keylight was changed shades of blue when the moon rise cue came into play; they were fitted with colour wheels that were also used in another show in that season's repertoire. This cut down on the re-rigging and repatching requirements and helped to speed up the turnaround. Corner three was mainly Lee 147 (apricot) as practicals cover for the summerhouse lights. Corner four was not used until the end of the show when the sun began to rise. This was in salmon pinks. There were in fact other practicals on this side of the stage so there was some more 147 to be used before the sunrise.

This formula worked well because the deep blues definitely gave the impression of darkness, but because the four different crosswashes were inconstant use, and constantly changing (lots of 10 and 20 minute fades going on), in terms of illumination the stage was actually quite bright.

More importantly the source and strength of keylight was always changing subtly throughout the show in order to prevent eye fatigue, which can be a problem in long dark scenes.

The End Of The Food Chain was considerably easier in that only a couple of scenes had the 'outdoor at night' treatment. Most of the show was set inside a warehouse, but occasionally the action took place on the roof. Again there was Supergel #68 for general cover with Lee 161 for moonlight and 147 for practicals cover (call me old-fashioned if you wish, but I used this particular colour combination a lot. It worked well for those atmospheres and provided good colour contrasts.)

What was interesting about these scenes were the angles of the keylight. Another myth about theatre-in-the-round is the lack of sidelight. My rooftop scenes in this show were keyed from 'moonlight' in a conventional cross-wash fashion like *Dreams From A Summerhouse*, but more predominantly from two low level sources.

One was a single Silhouette on a stand hidden within a seating block, which was shuttered and shot a shaft of light across the stage floor. This was intended as light through an open door and so was only used while the "door" was open. It was focused low to cast as much light as possible across the floor, and to avoid dazzling the audience in the opposite seating block, but was rigged high enough to get a perfect silhouette of the actors making their entrance: an integral part of the plot was that their identity is not revealed until approaching other characters already onstage.

The second low-level source was even lower and more dramatic. The roof top scenes were set with a truck appearing onstage with a skylight structure built onto it. The skylight was sloping clear perspex with a fan in the high side. There were Coda floods inside the truck illuminating the clear perspex from the inside. The high-pressure sodium type colours in use were very soft through this piece and worked well when the female character sat on the perspex and was lit from underneath. There was also a Birdie, a motor and a smoke machine built into the truck. The motor gently turned the fan, the Birdie lit through the fan, and the smoke machine periodically puffed 'steam' from this 'ventilation' fan. The light from the Birdie was lost into a void between seating blocks and the fan cast wonderful moving shadows across the actors, particularly when they were backlit by the 'door' light. The result was very atmospheric, the atmosphere being created by the mix of angles, colours, and just the right amount of smoke.

Neville's Island was again an outdoor setting (an island in Lake Windermere), and took place during all hours of the day and night. The night time scenes had similar treatment (dark blue, moonlight blue, but no 147!) but with additional keylight sources in the form of a passing ferry, a firework display, and plentiful use of miner's style head lamps worn by the actors. As my 'usual moonlight' formula interspersed with dusk and dawn worked for this show, the more interesting problem to solve was how to create the atmosphere of severe fog without resorting to copious quantities of smoke or haze.

Once again the Scarborough weather obliged and sent a sea-fret' during the design week, so I was able to take an afternoon out of the office in order to 'study' the fog – from the comfort of the harbour bar, of course!

The point about fog is that light is totally dispersed. There is no direction in the illumination at all. This contradicted my efforts in always trying to get direction and texture into each scene, but in this case I had to do my best to lose all sense of direction and keylight. I resolved this problem with various shades of daylight correction filters (which were in the general cover anyway), combined with the whole of the stage being lit by a battery of PC's focused directly downwards. This resulted in a very flat look with no discernable shadows or direction – exactly the 'look' that a lighting designer normally tries to avoid.

If the whole show had to be treated in this fashion, it would have been extremely tedious, but because there were plenty of other 'interesting' lighting scenes during the show the flat foggy scenes were acceptable interludes and worked well as a concept.

As a footnote, *Neville's Island* was to my knowledge the fifth show that involved real water on stage at Scarborough, so please don't think that theatre-in the-round is any more restrictive for set designers as it is for lighting designers.

Shows with water:

Way Upstream	Whole stage 'flooded' as a canal.
Time And Time Again	Garden pond with fountain
Man of the Moment	Practical swimming pool
Othello	Practical fountain – on a truck!
Neville's Island	Half stage flooded as Lake Windermere

Othello was lit by Mick Hughes and I remember it included lots of dark blues and straw. It is described more fully later in this book but I mention it because the production photographer had apoplexy at the darkness and had to send off to America for 3200ASA film!

I'm cheating by mentioning Macbeth here because I lit it at Harrogate Theatre, a classic Victorian proscenium theatre. However, it was arguably the darkest lighting I have ever seen! It is relevant because I treated it in exactly the same way as I would have had it been staged in the round. The general cover was very dark – Lee 180 (dark lavender) and Supergel #68 (sky blue), but with plenty of pale coloured shafts of light all over the stage, most of which were practicals cover. This gave the impression of a very dark place, but the actors could always find somewhere bright to be for their important speeches. My two favourite tricks were lighting from inside a sliding metal grid floor trap which created wonderful moving shadows through the smoke, and Lady M being lit only from reflected light from a pool of water for her "Out, out! Damn spot" speech. Yet again my theme of shadows and movement finds itself on stage. The point is not to be afraid of colour. Although this was a proscenium production, the colours, angles and contrasts would probably have worked better in-the-round because of the intimacy and ease of visibility in a smaller auditorium. Here's what Alfred Hickling had to say in the local paper review:

> "OH DARK, dark, dark: they all go into the dark." Thus T S Eliot in the Four Quartets and a neat summation of Andrew Manley's spectacularly black production of Shakespeare's murkiest tragedy.
>
> Macbeth is the play in which the bard most significantly failed to find the light-switch. It is one long invocation on the part of the central protagonists to be subsumed in smoky blackness.
>
> "Come thick night and pall thee in the dunnest smoke of Hell", "come, seeling night, scarf up the tender eye of pitiful day," exclaim the Macbeths (excellently portrayed by Peter Forbes and Catherine Prendergast), as if darkness were an ingratiatingly warm security blanket, guaranteed to keep one snugly insulated from the troublesome chill of cold-blooded murder.
>
> Lighting designer Jackie Staines must take a bow for creating the lowest-wattage lighting plot I have ever witnessed. It's terrifyingly good. Stumbling towards death in the primordial gloom, the deranged Macbeths become desperate for a spark of illumination.
>
> The sleep-walking Lady requires a feeble lantern beside her

always. She may as well attempt overdosing on carrots. Macbeth's farewell to life, "Out. out brief candle" has never been more chilling. Manley's production, hovering through the fog and filthy air, sets the action in a radio-active wasteland, opening ominously with the death-rattle of Geiger-counters.

Some people are going to hate this, and indeed if Shakespeare had any really strong thoughts on the subject of plutonium, he might have written a sonnet comparing his lover to a softly-glowing rock.

But Harrogate Theatre excel in the business of shaking audiences out of complacency: the standard of verse-speaking is exceptional, the characterisations consumate. The company succeed in casting new light on the play, having shrouded it in funereal darkness.

Using the Floor as a Canvas

It has already been shown how the floor can be used by the lighting designer in many different ways: for fun in The Village Fete, for effect in Mr A's Amazing Maze Plays, to give hidden depth in Gaslight, and to

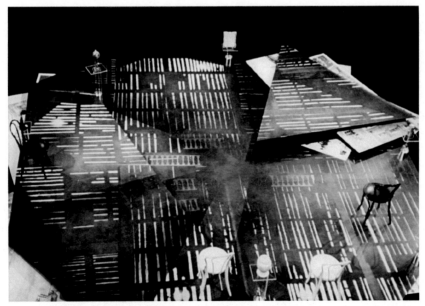

Photograph 16: 'Travels With My Aunt', Lighting: Jo Dawson, Set: Sue Condie, Photograph: Jo Dawson

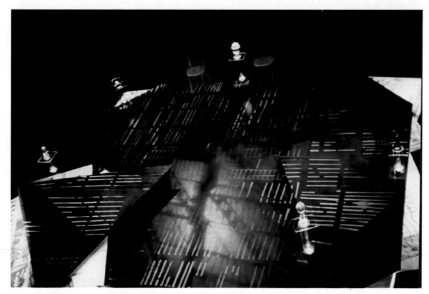

Photograph 17: 'Travels With My Aunt', Lighting: Jo Dawson, Set: Sue Condie, Photograph: Jo Dawson

create atmospheres with colours and gobos. In my conversations with other lighting designers, both Kath Geraghty of the Stephen Joseph Theatre and Jo Dawson of the New Vic Theatre, Newcastle-Under-Lyme mentioned the importance of the floor to lighting designers in theatre-in-the-round as it is often the only thing to light. Whereas in conventional staging formats the lighting designer can dress and enhance features on the set, the lack of conventional set pieces in theatre-in-the-round leaves the floor as the only available canvas for their art.

Apart from *Gaslight*, which was truly atmospheric, I have only used **Lighting for Fun examples** of my own shows in this chapter. For a more serious, or dare I say it, 'mature' approach to using the floor as a canvas, I am using Jo Dawson's New Vic Theatre production of *Travels With My Aunt* as a good example both of painting the stage and of liasing closely with the set designer and painters.

Jo mentioned this show several times during our conversation so I was not surprised that it was the one that she used as her example of a production that she was particularly pleased with. The set was a two level rostra painted with geometric patterns emulating light filtering through the cracks of a wooden barn's walls. She followed this idea through with the use of linear break-up gobos, but was also able to completely change the atmosphere of the show and the character of the floor by simple lighting changes. She worked closely with the design team when she chose her colours in order to enhance the depth and textures within the scenic art.

Photograph 17 also shows some of the perspex columns containing critical props located around the perimeter of the stage. Each column was lit from above and below - above by a narrow profile focused straight down, and from below and within the columns themselves. The two photographs here clearly show how radically a stage floor can be changed and Jo is understandably proud of this example. The designer quipped that the blue state had so much depth that "it looks like you could swim in it".

5 NIGHTMARES FROM ROUND STREET

Nightmares From Round Street

Almost every show comes up with some kind of difficult problem for the lighting designer or chief electrician to solve, regardless of the staging format. This chapter attempts to highlight some of those problems, and particularly those that are specific to theatre-in-the-round. Of course, much of what follows has already been introduced in earlier chapters.

Typical problems often arise from strangely-shaped sets, flying pieces, tall actors/short audiences, minimalist sets, multiple settings, cabling to practicals, shows with a static time span or location, and of course darkness. Another problem not strictly the concern of the lighting designer but definitely one for the chief electrician, can be trying to patch a lot of instruments into a few dimmers. This problem is of course venue-specific rather than typical of theatre-in-the-round but at Scarborough it was a problem of increasing frequency as lighting rigs grew. This chapter describes a few problem-solving anecdotes mainly from Scarborough, but they can also be applied to other venues.

Patching Large Rigs

If there is a guest lighting designer, patching large rigs can become a last minute panic. If you are resident chief electrician/lighting designer you can plan around this at all stages of the design process. At SJT (Westwood) I was frequently trying to patch up to 220 fixtures into just 60 dimmers. It can be done but it sometimes it isn't easy! You just have to think very carefully about pairing and about possible mid-show repatches. Observers would often ask me why I rarely looked at my rig plan during plotting and technical rehearsals but managed to accurately call the circuit numbers. The answer is obvious really – by the time you've designed the rig around the patch limitations, physically rigged it, patched it and focused it – it's as committed to memory as all your family birthdays. This is one advantage of having to contend with a hard patch – you are able to physically patch things in logical groups: general cover by area, colour washes, individual specials in scene order and so on. When you combine the electrician and

Photograph 18: Stephen Joseph Theatre (Westwood), one quarter of a typically crowded grid. Photograph: Jackie Staines.

designer roles you are constantly aware of all of these factors so it is quite easy to remember the rig. When SJT moved to the Westborough (former Odeon) building, the installation provided 240 dimmers so patch problems are now a thing of the past.

Finding Enough Positions

Of course big rigs also cause problems with physically hanging everything, particularly if the original grid plans are not particularly accurate. You draw the plan and everything fits but when it is rigged you will inevitably find a scaffold clamp exactly where that critical pin spot needs to be rigged. Composite gobos can also be problematic. Their image on the floor will be much more obvious than in proscenium so they need to be projected very accurately. The only way to do this (other than custom-designing a gobo set with key-stoning and distortion factors built in) is to rig the profiles as physically close together as possible. At Westwood there was just enough space above the bars to over-rig Pattern 23s so a five colour composite gobo effect was possible by rigging three lanterns below and two lanterns above the bar. In fact, the over-rigged lanterns would be too high considering that Pattern 23s are fixed beam, so the compromise was to spanner tighten them at a very peculiar angle to get their lenses as close as possible to the lenses of the conventionally hung lanterns. Manufacturers please note: can we have a high quality variable beam profile the same size (or smaller) than a pattern 23?!

As the rigs at Westwood grew progressively larger, so it became an issue when designing the grid for the new Westwood building, referred to during the design stage simply as 'The Odeon'.

For those readers not familiar with the Scarborough theatres, Stephen Joseph founded his company in a room above the Municipal Library. In the seventies, the company took the lease on part of a school building located and referred to as 'Westwood'. During my years at Westwood, the lease was approaching its renewal date so new premises had to be found.

In 1988, the Odeon cinema closed down and had remained empty ever since. It was falling into a state of disrepair and due to its prime location directly opposite the railway station, it was becoming known as the town's eyesore. This building later became the new home of the Stephen Joseph Theatre, after long negotiations with English Heritage over how much of the building could be gutted and rebuilt for its new purpose, and how much of it should be restored to its former Odeon Art Deco style.

The original architectual plans and model of the Odeon conversion showed a grid of catwalks, not dissimilar in style to the New Victoria Theatre in Stoke-On-Trent, often referred to as Scarborough's sister theatre.

Photograph 19: New Victoria Theatre grid, four catwalks and stage.
Photograph: courtesy of the Stephen Joseph Theatre Archive.

It was an obvious route for an architect to follow, especially when a project like 'the Odeon conversion' had never been tackled before. At this stage, the grid design was a provisional idea and was therefore open to suggestions and improvements.

I have to confess to not being very impressed by the model; there seemed to be an awful lot of catwalk and not much lighting space. I thought about this and figured that every place that supports a person steals a lighting position. I wanted the flexibility of being able to rig lights *anywhere* but also with maximum speed, comfort, efficiency, safety and convenience. Seven years of constantly moving spotlights and ladders in inconvenient or hard-to-reach places had taken its toll physically and what used to be 'fun' with a physical buzz had become a chore resulting in back pain. There *had* to be a solution.

I discussed this with Alan Russell of Theatre Projects Consulants and he suggested investigating a 'wire-mesh grid' originally designed by JR Clancy of New York. Research led to the Canadian company, Sceno Plus, who had installed these meshes in various performance venues in Canada and the US. The method employed is a wire mesh at high tension which can be safely walked on, with the lighting bars located above, and the lights shining through the mesh. Sceno Plus invited me to Montreal to see some of these 'trampoline' installations. It was the perfect solution; you could rig lights anywhere, you could stand up and work at a height that put no strain on your back. If you dropped a colour frame or barndoor it couldn't go anywhere so it was safe and prevented unnecessary breakages It was also radical and fun. We went for it.

Criticism of the system concerned the fact that the lights shine through the mesh and the mesh is therefore visible. Well, if the rig is exposed, which in theatre-in-the-round it naturally is, you can see the lights anyway, so that's not a problem. In fact, the mesh helpfully hides all the associated mess caused by the cabling and older ugly lanterns by providing a natural barrier between the rig and the rest of the auditorium.

Some theatre lighting professionals argue that the pools of light on the mesh are unsightly. However, these can be minimised by rigging the lanterns with their lenses as close to the mesh as possible in which case it is the same as looking directly into the lens. Realistically, audience members will have a good look at the rig before the show during the preset state, but once the show actually starts they are concentrating on the actors, not the lighting rig. If their attention wanders skywards during the performance, it is not the fault of the lighting rig – the director does have something more important to worry about!

What about shadows of the mesh? Yes, technically speaking the mesh does cast a shadow, but with the equipment rigged close to the mesh, it is so far away from the focal point that the shadow is indiscernible to the human eye. Technically there is a shadow: artistically there is not.

The Scarborough wire mesh grid is one of the largest installations of its type: it has a 'hole' in the middle to allow for large flying pieces, and spotlines can be dropped anywhere through the mesh. There must be some supporting joists in the mesh, but these can be interspersed with some of the wires at extra tension and at these points it feels as solid as a joist to walk over.

Periodically the wires need to be re-tensioned but otherwise it is a maintenance-free and flexible solution. It is also lightweight, which can be a structural consideration, and relatively cheap because it doesn't use much in the way of material.

Photograph 20: The Stephen Joseph Theatre, Westborough showing the tensioned wire grid with flying hole in the middle.
Photo: Sightline magazine, Autumn 2007.

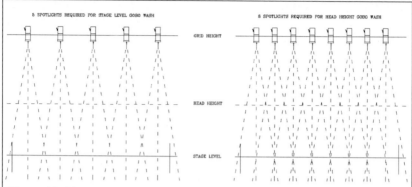

Figure 13: Using a section to calculate the number of spotlights required to create a head-height gobo wash.

Gobo Washes Galore

I have already mentioned the use of gobo projection several times: for setting scenes, as a substitute for scenery, and in the context of my habit for making my own. Habit? Sometimes because they were custom designs, sometimes because the budget did not spread to purchasing gobos (one show I have in mind required making 48) and sometimes for the sheer hell of it!

This quantity might seem somewhat excessive for such a small stage area (20' x 22')[11] but the quantity of gobos relates to another typical problem of theatre-in-the-round – short throw.

In *This Is Where We Came In*, a children's show with no set, various scenes had to be set by the lighting, including a forest at night and at day. This required two different whole stage gobo washes in different colours and angles. It was just about possible to cover the whole stage area with five wide angled Pattern 23s, albeit somewhat dimly, but this show also required 'corridors' of forest around the perimeter of the stage that had to be used independently to the rest of the stage. This involved the lanterns being focused virtually straight down and being carefully shuttered. It worked at floor level quite easily but of course would have left great dark holes at head height had the quantity of luminaires not been carefully calculated from section drawings. This in turn led to the usual problems

---

[11] 6.1 x 6.7 metre

Photograph 21: Stephen Joseph Theatre Westwood (during first season). The beam through the middle of the grid is clearly visible. In later years with larger rigs it became a great obstacle.

of where to hang them and how to patch them! I cannot stress enough the importance of sections and elevations. They're not always necessary, particularly if you are resident in a building and have learned the tricks of the venue, but taking the time to do a few simple sketches can save hours of re-rigging time.

Grid Obstacles

Stephen Joseph Theatre (Westwood) also had a unique problem in a that a rather large structural beam ran the length of the grid just slightly off centre, with six smaller beams at right angles to it. This made all rigs slightly asymmetrical and the beams constantly hindered the use of flying pieces and critical lighting angles.

Sometimes extra pieces of scaffold would have to be rigged around the beam to get equipment in exactly the right place, which was technically OK but ugly. In *The Village Fete* I had to rig a Cantata directly underneath the beam (shown dotted on the rig plan), but it was physically so low that

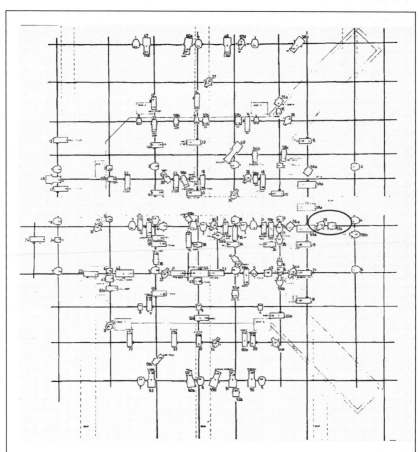

Figure 14: Cantata rigged under the beam in 'The Village Fete'

it was extremely obtrusive. If there had been a flying piece or raised stage area, I would not have been able to rig in such a position for aesthetic and safety reasons. Ideally a lighting designer shouldn't have to worry about peculiarities of venues in this way, but if you don't take them on board at design time, you can run into problems later and lose valuable time if equipment has to be re-rigged during the focusing session because you overlooked an obstacle. In the section ***Gobo Washes Galore***, I mentioned the method of over-rigging some of the lanterns used in composite gobos. This technique could not be used where the smaller beams were located in the ceiling so I made sure that the beams were always the first things to be pencilled onto my drawings. They also provided useful reference points for the rigging crew and can be seen in *Figure 14*.

The rig plan also shows the numerous profiles that were used for the 'groundplans of light', pictured in *Photograph 14*, and demonstrates how crowded the centre area of the grid around the beam can get. There would have been a bit more room for manoeuvre when rigging and focusing if that beam had not existed!

Size Isn't Everything

Several of my 'Nightmares' have been caused by shows requiring quite large rigs and the problems have been more to do with physically rigging and patching rather than actual design problems. The reader may well be left wondering why every rig was so large, but of course that was not always the case. *Haunting Julia* was the smallest rig I ever used on a show, yet just as effective as some of the bigger rigs. It also utilised a classic proscenium trick: the transformation scene – in a theatre-in-the-round!

The small rig was so small that it didn't even use the whole of the general cover. This was due to the shape of the set, which cut a diagonal across the stage. The square format of the general cover was not appropriate for

Photograph 22: 'Haunting Julia', Lighting: Jackie Staines, Set: Jan Bee Brown, Photograph: Adrian Gatie

the set because the diagonal cut off of the two halves of the set needed to be very well defined.

The show took place in a museum exhibition and the set was in two halves, the 'viewing area' and the 'set', so there needed to be a distinct difference in the lighting styles of the two halves of the set.

In order to create this distinction, 25 of the usual 36 Fresnels used for general cover were simply unplugged at the patch panel (they were left in the rig because the show was as usual in repertoire and the instruments needed for the rest of the season, so they are shown dotted on the plan). Some of them were replaced by ten profiles to get the diagonal cut off and these, along with what was left of the general cover, were left open-white to light the hardwood flooring viewing area. The 'set' half of the set was lit predominantly with dark-blue downlights and

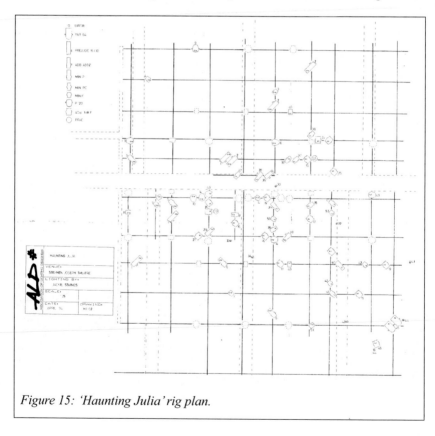

Figure 15: 'Haunting Julia' rig plan.

various tightly focused specials, emulating an 'architectural lighting approach' to lighting a museum piece i.e. the objects in the room were all individually lit, rather than by an even general cover for the actors.

This approach resulted in a patchily lit acting area but as it was a ghost story, it allowed the actors to move in and out of the shadows as appropriate. Unusually, I gave the actors a 'pep talk' at the beginning of the technical rehearsal to explain to them what I had done and why, and to make sure that they were aware of their keylights for their most important speeches. The actors were constantly moving in and out of atmospheric shadows, but were guaranteed never to be in the dark during key moments of dialogue. The atmosphere and required illumination was also helped by positioning four Birdies on the floor of the set which served two purposes: firstly the set designer had asked for light-fittings to be an integral part of the set, as you might see in an exhibit, and secondly, they provided spooky up-lighters for the scary bits! It was tricky finding places to put them where they would:

    a)   do a sensible lighting job

    b)   look as if they were an integral part of the set

    c)   not get kicked by the actors (or audience).

The whole concept was a good example of actors and designers working together as a team. (The Birdies were located next to the central pillar, next to the bed, and two underneath the desk. You can just see the latter three in *Photograph 22*).

More Birdies (what a wonderfully useful invention!) were used for the 'transformation'. The trick was probably not what the reader is expecting, but the technique and result were the same as a proscenium effect in that a gauze was used which needed to appear opaque for most of the action, but reveal hidden secrets at the right moment…

With reference again to *Photograph 22*, a seating block and vom entrance were removed and replaced with the wall shown at the back of the set. The door in the wall could open, but would only reveal a 'breeze block wall' behind it to the majority of the audience. The script referred to the fact that originally it was the doorway to the staircase but had been recently bricked up. No 'transformation' would have been necessary except for the few seats located behind and either side of the wall. For those audience members, there had to be no view inside of the wall until the end of the show. To achieve this, there was a horizontal gauze forming a 'ceiling' over

this part of the set. This ceiling was cross-lit just to give it some dressing and to make sure that it was completely opaque when the stage management team were inside doing their dirty deeds...

Without giving too much of the plot away, at the end of the show the door is opened and magically is no longer bricked up. At this point, the people in close proximity to the wall who for the duration of the show had endured the 'cheap seats' were treated to by far the best possible view of what happened inside!

Another example of using gauze was to hide some Birdies that were built into the set for *Love Off The Shelf*. The only permanent set piece was a large desk in the middle of the revolve. At the end of the show, the desk was transformed into an altar and the stage was covered in a thick layer of dry ice. I persuaded the set designer to replace two of the panels in the desk with similarly painted gauze panels and allow me to rig columns of Birdies behind them. These Birdies were invisible to the audience at all times but allowed two tricks: to light through the blanket of dry ice giving it a kind of incandescent quality, and to light a couple of bits of otherwise-impossible-to-get-at pieces of scenery, such as the cliff face (and actress) in *Photograph 23*.

*Photograph 23: 'Love Off The Shelf',
Lighting: Jackie Staines, Set: Jan Bee
Brown, Photograph: Jackie Staines*

Floor Surfaces

In some respects, the floor is the most important part of a theatre-in-the-round set. After all, not every set has doors, or furniture, or flying pieces but they do all have a floor of some sort. For the set designer, the floor is often the most important feature because it's their only opportunity to add something to the production. As a technician accessing the grid from stepladders you must always take great care of the floor because even if you survive the whole production week without scratching it, you will certainly get the blame when someone else does! Practically speaking, the floor can actually become quite a dangerous place. As soon as it is not level, or has rostra, or is slippery, or is grass or water… manipulating the ladder can become an art form. Care and speed are not often mutually compatible but on a dubious stage surface they have to be. Dragging of ladders is always forbidden, but sometimes extra care must also be taken. If the surface is particularly delicate, such as turf, then something must be put between the ladder feet and the stage. It doesn't sound like much effort but having to place four pieces of plywood down each time the ladder is to be moved adds up to a lot of lost time during a tight schedule. Similarly, if the floor is uneven, extra safety precautions must be taken to prevent ladder-toppling type accidents. Then if there are flying pieces as well, you have to watch what you're doing with the top of the ladder as well as its feet! Problematic floors are another excellent argument in favour of the tension wire grid method.

Artistically speaking, if a floor is shiny and/or at an angle there will be problems with reflections. Although this is also true in proscenium, if the viewing angle is only from one side, bounce and flare can be minimalised be changing the lighting angle. It is not that simple in theatre-in-the-round because if you cure a problem from one viewing angle you are likely to exaggerate it from another and will spend the entire production week chasing a reflection around the theatre!

If projection onto the stage surface is an important part of the lighting design, the stage must have a matt finish (please refer to the earlier example of *The Village Fete*), and ideally the final coat of varnish or PVA or whatever should be applied before the plotting session to prevent nasty surprises later in the proceedings. Shiny floors are not always a bad thing though; look back at *Photograph 10* of *Gaslight* in its preset lighting condition. The black gloss floor gave an enormous depth to the stage and the reflections of the boldly coloured lights added to the eerie atmosphere. Part of the floor was sloping – as if picked up and torn from the rest of the floor – which did cause a bit of a problem. During the first preview, there were five members of the audience who seemed to be rather brightly lit. It was quite strange because they were towards the back of the auditorium so it couldn't have been spill from something knocked out of focus. They looked quite yellowish but the majority of the lighting was in greens and blues. The following day I put up the main state for act one and sat in one of the offending seats. I was lit by bounce off the sloping part of the floor. It was caused by a combination of the angle of the slope and the angle of the three profiles that were reflecting onto the slope. It was a bit of a stalemate situation because the slope could not be changed, and re-rigging the three profiles would defeat their purpose. They were one of the main keylights on the set (window gobos) and it was critical that they light Mrs. Manningham when she stood looking out of the window located at the top of the slope, but also when she reclined on the chaise longue. To achieve that, they had to be rigged on the back bar of the grid, focused long and low. A lateral thinking solution was to ask the box office to sell those particular seats last!

Practicals and Problems

The vast majority of the shows I worked on at the Stephen Joseph Theatre in Scarborough had either practicals or hidden effect lighting, and often other miscellaneous electrics secreted around the set. These things are not unusual in themselves, but great care must be taken to keep the cabling both neat (i.e. hidden) and safe. It might sound obvious, but where you can get away with a taped down cable across a proscenium stage floor the same would be blindingly obvious to a theatre-in-the-round audience, particularly if they have to walk across the set to get to their seats. The only satisfactory solution is to bury the cables under the floor wherever possible. This is fine in repertory where the set stays put for several weeks, but a bit of a logistical nuisance when the show is in weekly or worse still, daily repertoire. Nonetheless this frequently happens and it must be dealt with whenever required.

Unfortunately, it's not just a matter of persuading the carpenter to rout cable channels into the floor; the chief electrician must also consider the nature of the turnarounds and liaise closely with the other departments over the order of work to be done. Where lighting grid access is by step-ladders, only the minimum of work can be done safely simultaneously be all departments. Whether the stage crew work late nights and LX early mornings or vice-versa will depend upon many factors and will vary throughout the season. How the cabling is built into the set can determine the order in which the work has to be done, so the whole turnaround scheduling must consider the cabling requirements. Excessive cabling at floor level can therefore become quite a burden on everyone, but must never be overlooked because of the risk of electric shock which always increases when the crew work long and unsociable shifts.

There are plenty of different examples of practicals and hidden effects, but the one thing that they have in common is that they are all time consuming, awkward and prone to breakages. That doesn't mean that I don't like them, I've seen some wonderful scenes involving the careful use of practicals; it's just that they are an inherent nuisance in repertoire because even when they're not in the way of your ladders on stage you are faced with the problem of storing them between performances!

Let's consider some examples, starting with the shows already mentioned. *Love Off The Shelf* was light on set and quite light on practicals. There was a battery powered miniature lighthouse (is it LX or props?) a battery powered candelabra, two dry-ice machines and the Birdies built into the desk. Neither of the battery-powered items caused problems: the lighthouse was turned on and off off-stage by stage management and the candelabra was given send-up treatment by being turned on and off in time to the music by the actors as part of the action. The dry ice machines were powered off stage anyway, but pipe ducts had to be built in underneath the seating.

The Birdies provided the biggest problem as they were rigged on the revolve. Ideally, a slip ring system should have been incorporated into the revolve but as it was an old existing mechanism that was built into the floor when the venue was first constructed, it was not possible to utilise such a system. Instead, loose cabling was fed to the Birdies through the centre of the revolve and the number of turns carefully plotted during rehearsals. Enough spare cable was allowed for the required number of rotations, and the revolve was 'unwound' after each performance and the loose cabling paged back in. Anti-snarl measures were taken and the cabling checked for damage every day, although as they were Birdies it was only low voltage cabling that was at risk from possible damage. The show was a straight four-week run, so there were no repertoire problems and in fact the cabling was left in for the following show (*Mr. A's Amazing Maze Plays*) which also utilised the revolve and required one circuit of Birdies.

Rocket To The Moon had several pendant light fittings and a practical fan hung from the grid. These types of practicals do not normally cause cabling problems because they are powered directly from the grid distribution. The only tedium is when there are a lot of practicals that might be tying up dimmer circuits that could be used for more artistic purposes. This show did utilise a desk lamp (shown in *Photograph 12*) but it and with the telephone were easy to cable because the banister rail hid the cables naturally, preventing the necessity of running the cables through the floor.

Dreams From A Summerhouse had two obvious sets of practicals which were used as warm wash keylights: the carriage lanterns on the outside of the summerhouse with apricot-tinted bulbs, and a set of festoons in the 'tree house' which was located on top of the main entrance and cannot be seen in *Photograph 9*. There was also some hidden effect lighting located inside the tree house and under the summerhouse decking floor, which transformed into dungeon scenes. Once again Birdies were used because their small size and intense beam were ideal for creating strong shafts of light emanating from the gaps between the planks. Ideally I would have liked wider gaps but Janie Dee was wearing stilettos so there was an ankle twisting injury risk to consider.

Gaslight was 'light' in terms of quantity of practicals, and caused no cabling problems in the weekly repertoire. The gaslight fitting was hung from the grid and plugged directly into a dimmer circuit. It was a small rig anyway so there were plenty of spare circuits available for this. The fireplace contained three Birdies on separate circuits. The Birdies themselves were in the fire grate and hidden amongst the coals, their cables passing naturally through the grate to their transformers located behind the fireplace. They remained bolted inside the fire grate for the whole season as they were not required for any other shows and they were cabled to separate circuits to allow for a gentle flicker effect of the fire.

Conversations With My Father was quite 'practical heavy'. Firstly, there were the numerous light fittings in the seating booths, the Birdies inside the flying piece, the juke box plus its speaker and some other practicals that cannot be seen in *Photograph 11*. The booth lights were all cabled back away from the stage, running within the seating blocks. The Birdies and the practical inside the flying piece, which in the photograph is hidden by the rouched curtain, took their power from the grid; in addition, there were ropelights inside the bar highlighting the shelves and glasses. These were discreetly cabled by routing in the underside of the false floor and the set was permanent for four weeks so once the cables were laid, they stayed put. There was nothing remarkable in any of this, but the cable management was very time consuming and therefore had an impact on the fit-up scheduling. Any show that requires a lot of practicals with tricky cable runs should be carefully considered at the fit-up planning meeting.

Neville's Island was set outside in the Lake District, so there were no lighting practicals. However, I mentioned earlier that the actors cooked sausages on stage. Due to fire regulations, we were not able to use a real camping gaz stove, so we adapted one with an electric element. We then had to run mains power underneath the set to a socket secreted within the stage floor. There was no problem with running the cable because part of the stage floor was raised by several inches. It just took a bit of dexterity from the actors to uncover the hidden socket and get the stove plugged in with the minimum of fuss. Self-contained gas would have been the better solution but as is often the case, electrics had to compromise due to outside influences.

The End Of The Food Chain had some Coda floods built into permanent pieces of the set, but there was also a truck that contained a Coda, a Birdie, a motor, and a smoke machine. All the cables, including the smoke machine remote control, were made up into a tripe and as the back end of the truck remained level with the vom mouth, it was acceptable to simply trail the tripe off behind the truck. If it came further on stage a more sophisticated cable management solution would have had to be found.

The four Birdies on the *Haunting Julia* set were rather delicate due to their propensity for getting kicked, and the addition of some rather flimsy home made barndoors. Their focus was also critical to, a) get the right effect, and b) not end up shining offensively at the audience.

The cables and transformers were happily secreted under the raised section of the floor, with conveniently located trapdoors enabling connection / maintenance access. The show was in weekly repertoire so after a couple of turnarounds the carpenter was persuaded into laying down the cables at the same time as fitting the floor, but no connections were required of him because of the trapdoors in the stage. Electrics were able to rig and connect the Birdies as part of the lighting turnaround the morning after the night-time set change. This arrangement worked well and I developed a taste for re-rigging at seven o'clock in the morning instead of during the night. Although with *Haunting Julia* the rig was so small that we could have done it any time!

Othello was an electricians' nightmare! I do not remember exactly how many practicals there were in this show but they were all temporarily rigged on trucks. There were truck tracks running across the stage from all three voms, and the truck from vom 1 had the ability to split in half. All four trucks had to have dimmable power for the plethora of lighting effects and other electrical items that were used throughout the show. It was my job as chief electrician (Mick Hughes was the lighting designer) to devise a method of getting power to the trucks in such a way that was discreet, safe, easy to replug the practicals, and, of course, cheap. I did it, but the method is more of a pub anecdote than a good example of working practices for a book.

There were numerous flicker-candles on various pieces of the set, including a rather splendid gilt map table (set design by Michael Holt). They were very realistic candles, but I don't think that they are manufactured any more: not flickering bulbs, but small 1W flame-shaped bulbs mounted inside an electromagnet. Periodically a pulse would be sent through the magnet causing the realistic flame bulb to sway gently in the 'breeze'. They were also the right intensity and colour to pass off as real candles and were very effective. The other notable electric feature was the fountain. It really was a small theatrical miracle that the thing:

a)   got on stage
b)   worked
c)   got off stage and out of the way of the exiting audience!

It was a large structure of plywood and MDF filled with water (obviously), so it was impossibly heavy and cumbersome, and it involved a six Volt fishpond pump. The knack was to start the pump at the right moment off stage so that the water fountain magically grew in front of the audience at the beginning of the scene once the truck was in place. It certainly got a few gasps of amazement during some performances and is arguably one of the best 'props' I've ever seen!

Abiding Passions had more good electric props. There were two 'oil lamps' that featured continuously throughout the show and posed a tricky lighting and electrical problem. They had to be completely portable by the actors, had to be turned on and off as part of the action, and they had to fade to blackout at the end of the act. Every lighting designer and electrician has experienced similar scenarios but how many times has an audience been fobbed off with a lamp or candle being extinguished by the flick of a battery powered switch? This method was clearly not acceptable for the drama of the piece, particularly with the proximity of a theatre-in-the-round audience that will always see and hear switches. To summarise the problem: the lamps had to be battery powered while they were being moved around by the actors, but they had to be powered from dimmers and controlled along with rest of the stage lighting at the top and tail of each scene. It presented a 'dual control' problem.

The solution involved, amongst other things: polystyrene, tinfoil, bent nails and a few 'real' components. This particular problem is one that could just as easily arise in other staging formats but one of the peculiarities of theatre-in-the-round is the proximity of the audience. They will see things that proscenium audiences cannot see, so in a proscenium theatre, our solution would not have needed such carefully chosen doilies...

The first part of the problem was portability. Simple enough – replace the wick with a bulb and stow batteries inside the oil chamber. However, the real problem was devising a way of switching the bulb from its internal supply to a dimmer, with no visible cables or switches. This involved a relay built into the oil chamber that switched between local battery and remote dimmed power, and a photo-electric cell to trigger the relay to switch at the right moment. The actors carried the lamps across the stage either unlit or lit under battery power, and then placed them on the set. Once in place, the actors would 'turn up' the lamp which would then switch from battery to dimmer power. The 'turning up'cue as well as a gentle increase in all the ambient light added a spotlight focused directly down onto the oil lamp. This was the only light in the whole rig that was shining directly on the photoelectric cell and was used as 'practical cover' and as the trigger for the relay switch. The oil lamp would remain on the dimmer supply until removed from its location, removal from the 'mains' supply causing it to automatically switch back to the battery power. If it remained in position, it was fully controllable by the desk.

Following liaison with the set designer, the lamps could only be placed on doilies in strategic places on the furniture. Each doily hid a polystyrene mat beneath it. The oil lamps had bent nails protruding from the underside of their bases, which stuck firmly into the polystyrene mats underneath the doilies. The nails then worked as pick ups from the 'electric doilies'.

Electric doilies? Where required, the polystyrene mats underneath the doilies were covered in tinfoil which was powered from a dimmer circuit via a six Volt transformer and cable running through the inside of the furniture. When a lamp was placed on a doily, the nails would penetrate the tinfoil before em-bedding in the polystyrene, thus picking up power from the six Volt tinfoil by no visible means. It was simple but effective and it worked for every single performance although we did replace the 'electric' mats each week – just as a precaution.

Man Of The Moment had no practicals in the true sense, but we were faced with the problem of making underwater cue lights for the swimming pool. We tried a few ideas, all of which worked, but actors being actors they got a bit over-sensitive about electricity-in-water and refused to use them. They failed to understand that the six Volt (homebuilt) cue lights are in fact a lot safer than the 240V (professionally built) underwater swimming pool lights used in the director's conservatory pool that they were happy to frolic around in. So much for our efforts – the cueing problem was resolved by the stage manager administering a sharp kick to the pool clearly audible to the submerged actor but not the audience!

The Musical Jigsaw Play was screaming out for an illuminated floor and moving lights, but the budget just wouldn't allow for them. The floor was divided up into four triangles, each one a pyramid-shaped jigsaw puzzle. All the jigsaw pieces had words rather than pictures on them, and the puzzle was solved during the show. When it was complete, each pyramid read a verse of a song but also all the words on all four sides when read in a spiral pattern also formed the song. By the end of the show, the audience would be singing the song that had emerged before them. Bring on the bouncing ball songsheet! Yes, with an illuminated floor we could have lit up each individual word of the song for the audience to follow. Budget, and indeed time, did not permit this idea, so the rig consisted of shuttered profiles focused straight downwards onto the words. With only 60 dimmers, there was no way it was possible to light each word individually (either from above or as an illuminated floor) so we compromised by lighting each line of each side of the puzzle individually rather than lighting every single word. Even so this still used up 24 profiles and 16 circuits, not leaving much equipment for other specials.

Once the song reached its climax, it had changed from a simple song sheet into a big rock & roll number. It had to be treated with as much razzmatazz as possible but without stealing too many resources from the rest of the show. After all, this scene only lasted for five minutes when there was an hour-and-half of drama beforehand to light in a suitably eerie fashion.

The 'number' used up 32 sub-kiloWatt PCs, four Parcans, four 1kW Fresnels and another 16 circuits. No wiggly lights for us, but a reasonable attempt at a four colour 'rock & roll rig' from the PC's and Parcans. A bit of nimble finger work on the Gemini flash buttons did the trick. (A Gemini – for rock & roll?!). To this day the musical director, John Pattison, remains one of my best friends, so it was important to me to make this thing look as lively as possible for his sake. The adrenalin of keeping his friendship provided the fire power behind those flash buttons!

I crammed the general rig into nine dimmers and patched all the floor circuits, which left me with an unenviable 19 circuits for real specials: real lighting.

Having got used to the idea that a bit of collaboration before the production can result in a mutually beneficial outcome (coping with the *Conversations With My Father* flying piece, using Birdies as an integral part of the *Haunting Julia* set, etc), the show's designer put her laser idea to me. The 'Bamboozler' (a strange talking robotic machine in the middle of the set) had to have smoke and lighting effects emanating from it throughout the show. Four coloured lightbulbs and similarly coloured Birdies hidden within it were driven by the Gemini's sound-to-light effect whenever it 'spoke', but there was also an idea that there should be a laser inside it producing many beams of light cutting through the smoke, or a moving light hidden inside.

Again, no money, no time, no space, no resources. By chance I found a large convex security mirror in a skip (Yes, by the end of 1994 my career was reduced to rummaging about in skips!). So I took it to the designer and asked if it could be incorporated into the Bamboozler. She wasn't too convinced until I rigged up a demonstration on stage of what I was thinking – a single Silhouette 30 rigged dead centre (structural beam permitting) and pointing straight down. It was fitted with a DHA Beam Splitter gobo and rotator (we already had the rotator and I did have the budget to purchase one gobo…) and focused onto the mirror. With just the right amount of smoke, we got the effect of multiple beams of light emanating mysteriously form the centre of the Bamboozler. It worked! The mirror was immediately incorporated into the set. If only the Sil could have been ten times brighter!

So there we have it. No illuminated floor, no moving lights (a couple of kk wheels though), no big rock & roll rig, no lasers, and just 60 dimmers. But the kids enjoyed themselves, and after all, that's what matters.

Calisto 5 was a technician's nightmare. Loads of practicals, pyrotechnics, video, live sound, virtually no equipment left for the rig *and*... in daily repertoire! Average working day: 7am to 2am (lucky) or 7am to 4am (unlucky) or 24 hours when things went really badly! Performances of *Calisto 5* were at 9:30am and 1:30pm, followed by the turnaround into *Taking Steps* (which also had loads of practicals and a grid full of specials) for a 7:30pm performance. After *Taking Steps* came another turnaround back into *Calisto 5* ready for the morning performance.

If *Haunting Julia* was a small rig, *Calisto 5* was miniscule, for a combination of reasons. *Taking Steps* had used most of the rig anyway and being in daily repertoire there was no time for a real re-rig between shows, considering the amount of work on the set turnaround. The show was lit by eight 1kW Fresnels and three Parcans on a total of seven circuits, but there were around 30 circuits of practicals to be run in at floor level. The set design of four 'control consoles' and a swivel chair made the acting area artificially small, so the eight Fresnels were adequate to light such a small area. When actors moved outside the main acting area – outside the consoles – it was natural for them to walk in and out of the light, and also desirable to be able to linger in the shadows. By giving the Fresnels a generous focus, there was enough ambient light for the actors to been seen outside the consoles, but only the centre area was properly lit in the true fashion, therefore minimalising the required resources. The show was

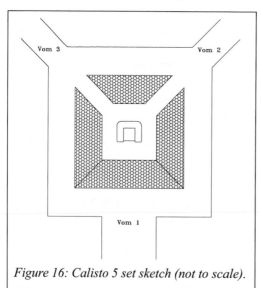

Figure 16: Calisto 5 set sketch (not to scale).

set on a space station, so I used daylight correction filters to achieve a cold, stark feel.

Each console contained numerous illuminating panels that needed to display different warnings at different times (a là Star Trek) which were powered by 18 ways of Pulsar portable dimmers built into the consoles. This prevented the necessity of an excessive amount of multicore running back to the dimmers' usual position (they were 'borrowed' from the Studio Theatre). The consoles also contained a large video monitor requiring mains and signal cabling, each capable of displaying one of four different video input signals as required; a loudspeaker for general sound, atmosphere, and video sound; and there were also 12 pyrotechnic circuits built in. The consoles and the floor which was laid on top of the *Taking Steps* floor were made of inch thick MDF and were somewhat on the heavy side. All this in daily repertoire!

The working day started at around 4pm when the *Calisto 5* performance finished:

1) De-power and disconnect all on-set electrics and remove remnants of pyrotechnics.

2) Remove video monitors, speakers, dimmers, and associated cabling.

3) Assist with removing *Calisto 5* set: partially as a 'goodwill gesture' to the all-female stage crew because of the weight and time restrictions, and partially in order to take mental notes of any damage that occurred to any of the electrics during the set removal procedure.

4) Re-patch from *Calisto 5* into *Taking Steps*

5) Re-arrange control room from *Calisto 5* into *Taking Steps* while the set is being placed.

6) Rig *Taking Steps* practicals – an arduous task of running cables under the carpet.

7) I run *Taking Steps* performances, my assistant goes home to sleep.

8) After *Taking Steps* Performance, strike practicals.

9) Re-patch from *Taking Steps* into *Calisto 5* and rearrange control room while *Taking Steps* set is removed.

10) Lay all *Calisto 5* cabling.

11) Assist with *Calisto 5* set.

12) Rig Video monitors, speakers, dimmers.

13) Set crew leave. Connect and test all electrics (pyros only with cabling

continuity test at this stage as we don't want to rig the pyros themselves until 8am).

14) By around 2am, everything is in place and, if we are lucky, working.

15) Work through night repairing anything that was trashed during the turnaround process. Sometimes this took all night.

16) My assistant arrives to help rig the pyros first thing in the morning. When her pre-show checks are done and she is happy, it's my turn to go home to sleep, unless any of the *Taking Steps* practicals need to be repaired in which case I work through first performance of *Calisto 5*.

17) Return at 4pm to start all over again.

The production period was hampered by a series of unfortunate events including freak weather conditions delaying delivery of the set and costumes, and a fire in the BT exchange disabling 50,000 local phone lines overnight. Propping is difficult enough as it is, but with an inoperable telephone exchange it's almost impossible!

Dear reader, take a moment to imagine life with no telephones, faxes, or email, and now try to imagine putting on a production under those circumstances.

Despite the trials of bad weather and bad phones, the initial filming was a success. A 'Lunar landscape' had been set up on the stage of the Crucible Theatre in Sheffield to film a robot's walkabout. On the same day, four monsters were also filmed. They were to appear in the 'video game' at the beginning of the show when Our Hero Jem is discovered shooting a toy gun at the video monitors. For audience members who remember the video game, I was in fact the second monster – the one with the long nose – and my claim to fame is that I was dressed entirely in cling film and bubble wrap! (Other monsters were the publicity officer, the casting director and the director's personal assistant).

I digress. What relevance 'bubble wrap monsters' you may be asking. The show opens with some rousing game music and young Jem (a boy stranded on a space station with only a neurotic robot for company), sat in the swivel chair. He is shooting a toy laser gun at the video monitors as the monsters randomly appear on the screens. The show climaxes with a similar shoot-out, but this time the monster is real but invisible (as opposed to being a video game). Jem has to shoot this monster but the only way it can be seen is through an infrared camera connected to the consoles' video monitors.

This whole sequence had to be filmed twice in situ, and because it had to be filmed and edited before the technical rehearsal, all the console electrics had to be rigged and working a full week before they are normally required for the technical rehearsal. It was critical that everything was working because the set would be seen on video, but in the story the video image a live image. Therefore what we saw live and what we saw on the video monitors had to appear to be exactly the same thing.

We experimented with a few ideas to get the finished video to look like an infra-red image and in the end we resorted in true theatrical tradition and used the cheapest, simplest and most effective method: a piece of Supergel #27 (medium red) Sellotaped over the camera lens!

To further complicate the issue, each time the gun was fired (which by the end of the show was no longer just a toy), a Pyroflash embedded in the consoles would be fired as the bullet hit. Because the video image was supposed to be 'live', the sequence had to be filmed with actress and pyros, replayed through the onstage monitors and filmed again without the actress (because the monster is invisible unless seen through the infra-red camera) and this second film played back in the show and timed perfectly to live pyrotechnics.

Music and sampled sound effects were all live so a video monitor was rigged by the side of the musical director. This part of the show had some heavy underscoring with a very strong rhythm. The MD was then able to follow and play the music to fit the original video and the pyrotechnics and shooting acting were all cued from the rhythm of the music – devious but it worked. It really did seem that the pyrotechnics on the video were the same as the live pyrotechnics being fired during each performance. Actually it didn't matter too much because by the time the twelfth one went off it was so smoky that you couldn't see the video monitors anyway!

The show also involved a live off-stage voiceover (by the same actress that was the invisible monster), so a microphone, show relay, show CCTV and video feed all had to be fed to somewhere sound proof. The building was shared with Scarborough Technical College so noise was often a problem from overhead or the blocked-off stairwells. There wasn't anywhere sound proof but the artistic director's office was usually very quiet, so we set up camp in there. It meant more equipment and cabling had to be laid in temporarily for this show, and it caused great inconvenience to the real users of that office.

The set and lighting for *Calisto 5* could have been stunning, but trying to do it in daily repertoire was not a good decision considering the construction of the set and the technology involved. If it had been a static set for a straight run, we could have been far bolder and braver with our special effects.

Feed was a great show, with a small cast and an interesting set. It is a musical drama about the lives of two music hall performers and spanned many years of their working lives. There were two aspects to the lighting design: many scenes were naturalistic, such as those set in the dressing room and the nursing home, whilst others were flashbacks to their music hall performances and had to be treated as such. To assist with this illusion, there were lightboxes around the edge of the 'stage', and various lengths of ropelight. The practicals were all powered from the studio dimmers and multicores were run in underneath the auditorium and raised part of the stage area, so not a single cable was visible. A sketch of the *Feed* set is shown in *Figure 20*.

Flying Pieces and Tall Actors

Elevations, Elevations, Elevations! We have already seen how it is necessary to draw a section when first dividing the stage into acting areas to calculate the number of required instruments, and also for achieving a gobo wash. These drawings (even if they are only rough sketches) are also needed when flying pieces are involved in the action but can be seriously useful for trivial sounding things such as a particularly tall actor. The

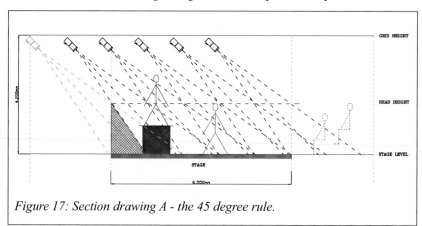

Figure 17: Section drawing A - the 45 degree rule.

worse possible scenario is a combination of a tall actor, a short audience (children), rostra and a flying piece! *Figure 17* demonstrates this.

The diagram demonstrates a number of points. Firstly, the example shows how the general cover is built up. The dimensions of this 'virtual venue' are reasonably typical of theatre-in-the-round and very similar dimensions are found at all three Stephen Joseph Theatre venues and the Old Laundry Theatre in Bowness-on-Windermere. What is not typical is the use of 30° profiles used for general cover. More commonly Fresnels are used for the general cover but I have also come across Parcans (The Rose Theatre) and profiles (Cottesloe and New Vic Theatre, Stoke), so you need to be prepared for these situations.

In the chapter ***Designing General Cover*** it was established that venues of these dimensions can typically be covered in nine stage areas (three rows of three), but that was only by using fully flooded Fresnels. *Figure 17* shows that by using instruments with smaller beam angles, the rig quickly doubles in size and achieves very little other than using up all the instruments and all the circuits!

The diagram shows one side of the cover, so it will be duplicated on the other three sides, at a somewhat mathematically placed 45° angle. The standing green man is a scale representation of an average height actor, so his head height is shown by the horizontal dotted line. To light his face across the whole width of the stage at a 45° angle using 30° instruments will require five rows of acting areas. Although his face is lit, when he stands on the left edge of this stage, his body is in shadow and there is a nasty dark patch on the floor, (remember, the floor is the canvas), so I have added a sixth instrument (the blue one) to fill in this hole. Unfortunately a six-by-six pattern of cover will not allow me the possibility of fading down to the centre area on its own, as this pattern of general cover does not form a central area. It is not strictly necessary to have a central area but it can be useful, and if you know from the blocking that it will be necessary to light the centre separately then this must be taken into consideration when designing the general cover.

There are three ways of correcting this error based on *Figure 17*. We can add another row of instruments on each side to give an odd number and therefore a central area, we can cheat and stick with the six-by-six pattern and add an extra central area on top of it, or we can reduce the cover to five by five to get an odd number and central area. I choose the last option.

- Option one: A stage of 7 x 7 acting areas is somewhat excessive – 49 acting areas lit from four sides, equals 196 instruments. Unless it's Wembley Arena forget it!

- Option two: 6 x 6 acting areas plus an extra central area – still a somewhat massive 148 instruments. Imagine how crowded that grid will be.

- Option three: Reducing to a 5 x 5 pattern – results in a more manageable 100 instruments, permitting a huge saving in cost, time, equipment, weight loading, power requirements and space by using fewer wider angled instruments. There's still a big difference between 100 profiles for this method and 36 Fresnels required by the nine areas method, but if only profiles are available, a 5 x 5 stage area must be used.

OK, so life is a compromise and in this example we are stuck with 25 areas each lit with four profiles. How do we achieve this when the diagram clearly shows that 36 areas are required?

The problem is solved by breaking the 45° rule. Like most rules it's there to be broken, and it was only ever intended as a rough guide anyway. Looking back at the diagram, we lose the sixth (blue) instrument altogether and then have to respace the remaining five. In the late 1950s, Stephen Joseph had already stipulated that the angles should vary across the rig. In the diagram there is an awful lot of spill into the audience, and if our man sitting in the front row was a child, he would be blinded. To prevent this, the instrument on the right hand side of the diagram needs to be focused at a steeper angle. The next one to the left will have to be tweaked to angle somewhere in between that of the centre instrument remaining at 45° and

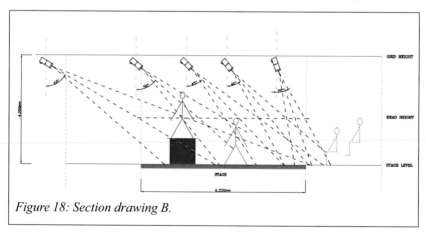

Figure 18: Section drawing B.

the steeper focused fifth instrument. Similarly, if the first (black) instrument on the left is rigged further away from the stage and coming in at a flatter angle, it will cure the dark triangular shadow at the edge of the stage and instrument number 2 is tweaked to fill the gap between 1 and 3. The result is a progressive change of beam angle across the whole rig.

The problem has been solved, but there are pros and cons to this. At head height, the green man is evenly lit across the whole stage, but the floor becomes patchy. The floor at the far right is lit by all five instruments whereas there is still a small black whole on the left. This is counterbalanced when the wash from the opposite direction comes into play, and the stage floor will be evenly lit. However, you now have an apparent discrepancy in the areas at head height and stage height. Be very careful during plotting and when talking to the director and designer. What you understand to be 'Area 4' and what they see as 'Area 4' will be perceived differently. This becomes even more apparent when you get into pin spot' specials. A nice, neat head and shoulders spot becomes a four-foot splodge on the floor in a different actng area. You have been warned – no matter how hard you try you cannot break the laws of physics and organise for the light to stop miraculously when it hits an actor!

So averaged height green man is well lit wherever he stands and 'our kid' in the front row is comfortably dark. But what if green man is taller, or does what pink man is doing and stands on a desk - not an unreasonable thing to do in an average comedy. If we're lucky pink man will still be lit by the general cover, as in the diagram, but if the desk or rostra were positioned a little further to the right, pink man would only be lit from the chest downwards because his head is between rows of general cover so extra fill lights must be rigged to cure this problem.

As we saw earlier with *Rocket To The Moon* and *Conversations With My Father* it is also essential to use sectional sketches when there are flying pieces in the set, or even to help position practical lamps' cover. So if you are ever faced with the fatal combination of tall/high actors, short audiences and flying pieces you must uses sketches in order to prevent a lot of grief after the technical rehearsal.

Walls, Stairs and Voms

In addition to the general cover, it is also usually essential to light the entrances well. *Photograph 7* in Chapter 2 clearly showed contrasting

front and back vom lights but in addition to these 'conventional' entrances, 'surprise' entrances can be made down various auditorium staircases. This is a notoriously difficult and frustrating task which can use up an incredible amount of equipment. Once an actor is standing more than half way up the stairs, the throw from the grid is minimal so a lot of instruments are required for even cover, front and back. The instruments must be well shuttered or barndoored to keep spill off the surrounding audience and are therefore not working efficiently due to the resulting light loss from such harsh shuttering.

If all three voms and all five staircases in the Stephen Joseph Theatre (Westwood) needed this treatment, there would be almost as many lanterns lighting off stage as on. It is sometimes very frustrating to have to use up so much equipment before specials can be considered.

What a mess! Look how horribly flat the angles are towards the top of the stairs: the last front light is at 78° – way off the desired 45°. To bring the light all the way down the stairs, instruments at flat angles must be carried on to the grid area over the stage, their beams cutting through the steeper beam angle of the outer edge of general cover. This results in an unavoidable and noticeable change of beam angle as the actor steps from stairs to stage. Backlight is somewhat easier because the beam is lost naturally down the stairs anyway, but unless there is height to over-rig a luminaire on the back bar, backlighting someone at the top of the stairs is virtually impossible.

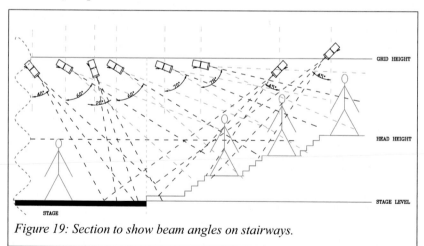

Figure 19: Section to show beam angles on stairways.

But these obstacles also have their advantages. One of the criticisms or observations that 'proscenium people' have about theatre-in-the-round is the absence of sidelight positions. This is not strictly true. If you want strong sidelight or low-level angles, you can make them. For want of self-praise, I did manage to make a habit of squeezing small things into small spaces and as a result adjectives such as 'deep' and 'textured' were often used to describe my design work, both by myself and by others. This was achieved by using to my advantage the very things that caused problems, although the poor old auditorium became so full of holes that I was banned from doing it for a while!

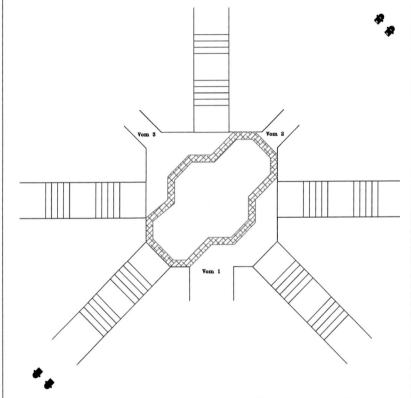

Figure 20: Sketch plan of 'Feed' set showing diagonal washing Parcans in far corners of auditorium. The red outline of the set marks the lightboxes creating a partially illuminated floor.

Using *Feed* as an example again, I wanted strong, brightly coloured side lights for the music hall scenes. The shape of the 'stage' cut a diagonal across the stage area and created a very natural proscenium stage shape. I wanted to light along the length of this diagonal at a low as possible level, as if it were sidelight coming from the wings of a proscenium. I rigged Parcans in the very back corners of the grid, shooting off to the opposite diagonal, and supplemented these with a more conventional 'cross-wash' of PCs in the same colours. The Parcans were at such an angle that ordinarily they would have blinded the audience members opposite, but the spill from these was conveniently lost down a vom in one direction and up a staircase in the other. The actors benefited from the effect of strong music hall style sidelight but no damage was done to the audience.

Voms, stairwells and walls are more than just places to lose excess spill. They can be used as useful, low level and discreet rigging points, and many a fixture has been bolted on top or underneath a vom roof, to a vom wall, or even inside the staircases with discreet peep holes cut in to them.

If I were given the opportunity of helping to design a new theatre-in-the-round, I would push for open or semi open risers on the staircases so that every step became a potential rigging point! With reference to *Figure 20*, notice how every 'low level rigging point' is directly opposite another one (stair/vom, stair/stair) so low level lighting is always harmlessly lost into a dead area and therefore does not discomfort any audience member.

If I dare use the 'Birdie' word one more time, they are perfect for these situations because of their small size. In *Two Weeks With The Queen* I had six of them on top of vom 2 and 3 roofs, complete with miniature colour scrollers.

The Beauty of Symmetry

The Musical Jigsaw Play, despite all its frustrations, did result in a beautifully symmetrical rig plan, especially when it transferred to the Old Laundry Theatre in Bowness-on-Windermere where the grid really is square instead of being disrupted by the structural beam that has blighted so many Scarborough productions. I'm not suggesting that aiming for symmetry is the 'right' or desirable thing to do; it's more a conversational point because in my seven years in theatre-in-the-round it was the only time it ever happened – the reason being that there weren't any 'real' specials. There was a formula involved for lighting the floor, lighting the band and

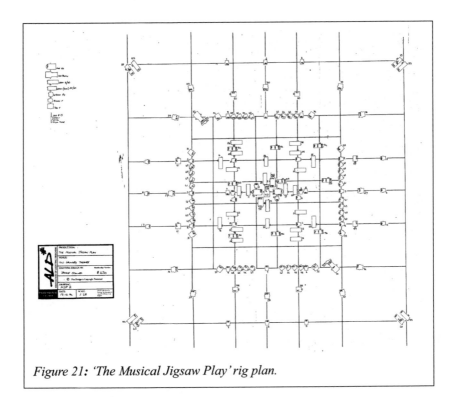

Figure 21: 'The Musical Jigsaw Play' rig plan.

lighting various bits of the set, but the set was symmetrically square and so the formula was repeated on all four sides. Result: perfect symmetry! The four banks of PC's that were used for the 'rock & roll' lighting can be clearly seen around the perimeter of the stage (see *Figure 21*), in Supergel #370 (Italian blue), Supergel #22 (deep amber), Supergel #49 (medium purple), and good old fashioned open white.

The counter side of this point is how to deal with lack of symmetry as I experienced on *Two Weeks With The Queen* when it played in the Cottesloe at the Royal National Theatre. There were many potential problems in taking this kind of show in this staging format into this particular venue, but the Cottesloe was surprisingly forgiving and needn't have caused so much worry after all.

The most obvious difference between the Cottesloe and Scarborough and Bowness is that the Cottesloe is not a purpose built theatre-in-the-round. It is usually in an end stage format, but also makes a good traverse. Turning

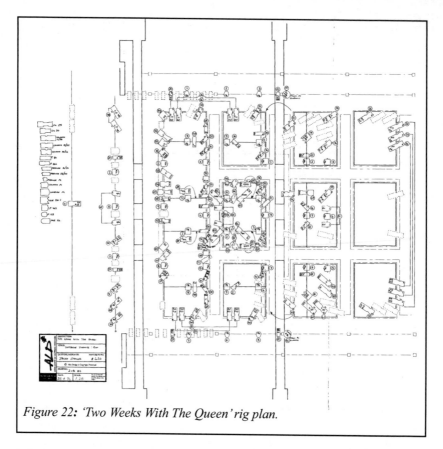

Figure 22: 'Two Weeks With The Queen' rig plan.

it into a theatre-in-the-round is a bit of a compromise and it can come in for some criticism when it is used in this format.

A venue such as the Stephen Joseph Theatre is designed to have an equal number of seats at similar angles on all sides. There are no 'cheap seats' and theoretically any viewing point is as good as any other. In the Cottesloe, two sides have around six or eight rows of Bleacher type seating, and the other two sides have three rows of temporary 'classroom' type chairs. However good the direction, the people in these latter positions will feel that they have the 'cheap seats' because of their temporary nature and this creates an uneasy 'us and them' feeling amongst the audience.

From the lighting point of view, the rig is even more obviously designed for an end stage format. Two-thirds of the grid is made up of 'egg crate' type catwalks, and the stage end third by conventional flying bars. There are two quite low bars running either side of the auditorium which provide side light in a thrust format so the result for theatre-in-the-round is three different lighting styles for the same job.

The rear egg crates are equipped mainly with Cantata profiles, the centre egg crates contained a mixture of equipment, the flying bars 1kW profiles and 2kW PCs, and some Pattern 123s were used on the low side bars.

In Scarborough and Bowness the general cover was made up of 4 x 500W Fresnels on each area of the stage. At Rose Bruford College it was 3 x Parcans plus a Fresnel to fill, but in the Cottesloe, each area was lit with a mixture of 2kW and 1kW profiles, 2kW PCs, 1kW and sub-kiloWatt Fresnels with assorted beam angles. It was not possible to change these instruments because they all made up the Cottesloe general rig and were in weekly repertoire with shows in other staging formats.

The number of available dimmers was not vast and because *Two Weeks With The Queen* involved quite a large rig, all four instruments focused on each area had to be paired together. I ordered extra neutral density filter thinking that there would be an intensity problem in matching 2kW Cadenzas to aging Pattern 123s but surprisingly, due to the throw distances, all the instruments were well matched in brightness at stage level and the neutral density was not required. Maybe the Cadenzas were dirty and the Pattern 123s had been freshly scrubbed!

Further problems were encountered with the actors' entrances. They were not really tunnels like the voms in other venues, and they were not at 45° diagonals from the stage corners. Vom 1 was OK, straight through the middle of a seating block, but the other two were fomed from corridors running up the sides of the seating blocks, so they were almost impossible to light into, and totally impossible to light out of. But then multipurpose venues are always a compromise.

6 LIGHTING DESIGNS IN THE ROUND

Design Examples From Others

Up to this point, most of the examples in this book have been taken from my own experiences as a lighting designer, as a chief technician, in conversations with Alan Ayckbourn or research into the work of Stephen Joseph. In seven years, I gained a fair amount of experience of lighting this particular staging format, but there are many other people who have, or are working in-the-round. To broaden opinion, I discussed the subject with several leading lighting designers working in the field and am pleased to be able to include the following commentary.

Mick Hughes, Lighting Designer

Mick Hughes has lit many of Alan Ayckbourn's shows in London, but first came to Scarborough in 1989 to light the epic five hour show *Revenger's Comedies*, his first design for theatre-in-the-round. Mick and Alan Ayckbourn – and the set designer Roger Glossop – had often worked together as a team on Alan's productions in London, but *Revenger's Comedies* was the first time the team had set foot together on the Scarborough soil – or perhaps I should say sand! Being used to major London theatres and Alan's professionalism, a dingy converted school hall certainly came as a shock to the two designers, but they soon settled down into making the best use of the available resources. Mick was not accustomed to having to compromise a design for the benefit of a repertoire season, but he wasn't adverse to the idea of using the general cover once he had seen it and walked through it to get a feel of how the cover, and the acting area, worked. *Revenger's Comedies* is two full length plays that can be seen on separate evenings, or as a double bill on a matinee day. It has multiple settings and requires rapid scene changes. The first challenge for Mick and Roger was to recreate Albert Bridge across half of a 20 foot stage – convincingly!

But that was just the start of the show, and action also took place in a café, the house and grounds of a country estate including animal stalls, and in other characters' homes. There was also a very complex sound plot and as chief technician I would be operating. I was therefore quite glad that Mick would be faced with the problem of cow sheds and sow stalls!

As the lighting designer, Mick was more than capable of creating all these different atmospheres, but what came as a shock to him was the patch – having to cram around 220 luminaires into 60 dimmers. It was a shock for me too, because I'd never seen such a big rig in this small venue before! Mick devised a wonderful 'patch table' that showed at a glance which dimmers were used for which specials and therefore when mid-show re-patches could take place. What it didn't account for, and quite rightly, was the fact that whenever there was an available time for re-patching it coincided with a complex sound sequence. In those days at Scarborough, there was a 'single operator policy' which meant that I would be operating both lighting and sound on this mega-show, so I had to rethink his patch plan. It was not all logistically possible, so in the end I had to 'negotiate' with the stage manager and arrange for an ASM to dash up the stairs to the dimmer room and do a couple of the mid-show re-patches for us.

As the production week progressed, Mick warmed to our little 'black box' theatre and the team was established. There were to be many more Ayckbourn/Glossop/Hughes alliances in Scarborough, both at the old and new venues.

He returned the following year for another Ayckbourn premiere: *Body Language*. The show was set outdoors in the grounds of a hospital and required suitable outdoor style lighting. From a lighting designer's point of view, this is quite a straightforward show, the only difficulties in our production arose during focusing because the three foot high artificial grass slope made ladder access difficult. Far more challenging for Mick was his next Scarborough project, *Othello: The Play*.

This Ayckbourn adaptation of the Shakespeare classic led to some controversy at the time due to the casting of Michael Gambon in the lead role and the use of a lot of dark make-up. On this occasion the set was by Michael Holt rather than Roger Glossop and some of the pieces such as the map table and the fountain (both described in the chapter **Nightmares From Round Street**) were absolutely wonderful – if a little large!

Mick ventured into the darkness for this production and, if I remember correctly, the whole general cover was Supergel #68 (skyblue). Cutting through this were splashes of Lee 103 (straw) and 147 (apricot) providing good contrasts and modelling qualities. There was a lot of dappled light as well from various breakup gobos including Moroccan meshes and home-made palm leaves. It was a tricky piece because there was so much richness in the set and costumes but a lot of darkness in the atmospheres. Mick was quite surprised at how dark Alan wanted him to take things during plotting, and the production photographer was not best pleased at the challenge it gave him. However, my memory of this show is not one of darkness, but one of texture; and the set, costumes and lighting all worked well together to achieve this balance and atmosphere. It was another example of good team work from the designers.

In my time at the Stephen Joseph Theatre, Mick Hughes also lit *Wildest Dreams*, *Taking Steps*, *Time of My Life* and *Communicating Doors* – all Alan Ayckbourn shows and also *One Over the Eight* directed by Ayckbourn. Each show brought its own set of challenges and it was always interesting to see how Mick would tackle them, and how similar (or otherwise) our lighting-problem solving instincts were.

Wildest Dreams is a strange tale of intertwining friendships. The characters are a group of friends who regularly play a Dungeons and Dragons type game, and the plot follows through their role-play with their fantasy characters. The set was divided into three distinct areas, representing different characters' accommodation and had to be lit as individual sets. As is often the way with Ayckbourn plays, there was a good sprinkling of night-time scenes and in this case, Mick had to represent the orange glow of sodium steetlamps through windows. I had a good look through my swatchbooks to see if I could work out what colour Mick would use for this. As it turned out, he used two colours rather than one, and this mixture provided the perfect representation of low pressure sodium. I can't mention the colours here because it's not my secret to give away. However, I used the same colour combination myself when I was faced with a similar street-light scene. Later I confessed to Mick that I had stolen his idea, to which he replied: "Doesn't matter, I nicked it off Mark Henderson and he nicked it off someone else!". So it just goes to prove that nothing is original – if you see it on stasge, it's been done before!

The production of *Taking Steps* that Mick lit was a revival and ran in daily repertoire with another Ayckbourn show: *Calisto 5*. Both shows had many practicals and the turnaround between them was not easy. This is discussed earlier in the **Nightmares From Round Street** section of this book.

Time of My Life is one set, but several timezones. Many shows take place over an extended time period, such as *Conversations With My Father, Same Time Next Year*, etc but usually time runs chronologically. Not so with *Time of My Life*, or indeed *Communicating Doors* where the plots jump both backwards and forwards through time. In these cases, it is important for the lighting to work in sympathy with the set and costumes,and nd to ensure that any time delineating differences in style are maintained throughout the duration of the show.

Communicating doors opens with a searchlight effect. How would a West-End and National Theatre lighting designer such as Mick create such an effect on a small stage with an even smaller budget? Pancan? Vari*Lite? Golden Scan? followspot? Pattern 23 on a swivel bracket pulled around by a piece of string and elasticated to make a return... Yes. Sometimes the simplest and cheapest of solutions proove to be the most effective, and Mick was always willing to try out workshop experiments to find solutions to his lighting problems.

Mick Hughes came back to Scarborough every year to light an Ayckbourn show, and the tradition continued into the new building where the Hughes/Glossop alliance came together for the first show in the new building, *By Jeeves*.

Unfortunately I have not had the opportunity to discuss *Othello* and *By Jeeves* directly with Mick, but I am hoping to expand upon his 'Scarborough experiences' for the next edition of this book.

Kath Geraghty,
Senior Technician, Stephen Joseph Theatre

Kath Geraghty joined the Stephen Joseph Theatre in 1994 where she worked as my assistant on *Gaslight, Haunting Julia, Penny Blue, Two Weeks With The Queen, Conversations With My Father, The Musical Jigsaw Play* and *Oleanna*. Her first experience of the Old Laundry Theatre in Bowness was to re-light *Jigsaw*. The following season she continued after I left and is currently Senior Technician for the Stephen Joseph Theatre. I was interested in her comments for this book because she has worked both as a technician and a lighting designer in the Westwood building as well as The Round (former Odeon) and Bowness and Stoke, and can therefore make direct first-hand experience comparisons between the different venues.

Kath and Mick Hughes between them tried rotating the general cover through 45° so that it is was keyed from the corners rather than the sides. The stage was still divided into nine areas, but the angle of 'attack' was different. They decided that they preferred this as more members of the audience got to see two 45° angles rather than one 90° angle, but as Kath says, she always uses the two colour 'steel and straw' approach to the general cover, so this viewing angle becomes important to

Photograph 24: Kath Geraghty at work in the technician's office at the Stephen Joseph Theatre. Photograph: Jackie Staines

achieve the modelling from the two colour method. When the company moved to the new venue, the general cover was designed around this pattern, still using a basic 36 lanterns, but this time 1.2kW Fresnels. This cover is supplemented with four lanterns into each vom (two colours each), plus 12 Fresnels with scrollers to provide an all purpose colour wash, totalling 60 luminaires for the general rig. The move from sub-kiloWatt to 1.2kW was to compensate for the extra throw (the grid is higher in the new building than Westwood) and for lighting through the mesh which does absorb some of the available light.

One of the drawbacks of working for the majority of the time in one venue is the tendency to develop lazy habits. You find a particular formula that works and then keep applying it over and over again. A certain angle, a certain colour combination, a certain method for creating colour washes, and so on. I am certainly guilty of formulating all of these things: as the adage goes, "If it ain't broke, don't fix it", so if a method worked well on one show it is likely to work on others. I questioned Kath about the possible development of any habitual routines.

Like all designers, she is always looking for new approaches to problems but she confessed to settling into a basic pattern of a four-sided general cover plus a three-sided colour wash using scrollers. This could have been an ideal all-purpose solution, but she is limited in only have 12 scrollers and it's not possible to satisfactorily cover the stage area with only 12 luminaires. Eventually they ended up forming a ring around the perimeter of the stage.

Kath tried to break this habit after a show that she was not particularly pleased with. The formula had been used to provide general illumination for the show, but it asked for little else either from the script or from the direction. The result was that she felt the lighting was very flat, and the colour washes just didn't work because there was an intense pool of colour in the centre of the stage but nothing at the edges.

For the summer season 2000, Kath experimented by attempting to use fewer luminaires for the basic cover but also to improve the integrity of the wash. She is doing this by reducing the cover from four-sides to the 120° rule, but it appeared from our conversation, that she was not particularly pleased with the results. There are three basic reasons for her scepticism with this method: throw, angle and colour.

Bearing in mind that the grid at SJT (Westborough) is higher than the Library, Westwood or Bowness, the distance between the three luminaires into each acting area and the throw from the instruments to the stage floor is just that much too far. One of the beauties of smaller auditoria (remember Stephen Joseph's ideal theatre-in-the-round should have no more than six rows of auditorium seating) is the subtlety in plotting levels. It is not uncommon to be plotting at levels between 25% and 35%, and Kath enjoys the effect of this on the colour temperature to "make things cosy". When there are only three instead of four lanterns focused onto each acting area, the levels need to be plotted a little higher to compensate for 1kW per area being lost, which in turn prevents the ability to use a low colour temperature advantageously.

The 120° angle forces the three luminaires to be placed a very long way apart and combined with the relative steepness of angle, Kath is very conscious of a 'kind of lumpiness' in the cover; it just doesn't cover as smoothly as a four-sided wash. Although she has not used this method at Bowness (Mick Hughes has), she suspects it works better in smaller venues where the difference in angles between the lamps is less obvious.

Using 120° also prevents the successful use of a two colour general cover (as opposed to a two colour wash) because there will always be an

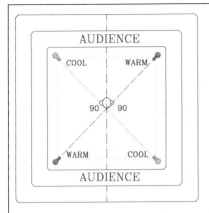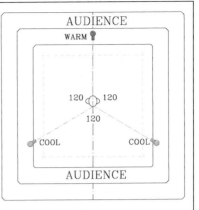

Figure 23: Sketch showing the use of a two colour general cover at 90° and 120°.

odd lamp in an odd colour which can be perceived to be a backlight. This could actually work quite nicely, if the actor only ever faced one direction! When he does not have his back to the odd coloured instrument, it would look more like a mistake than a deliberate design policy. Kath prefers the four-sided approach because of the way in which she likes to colour the general cover.

The new venue for the Stephen Joseph Theatre was virtually custom designed as opposed to being a conversion of an existing building. Although the basic building is old and the auditorium placed inside the existing shell, unlike the previous locations, it was completely gutted and the theatre-in-the-round part was designed from scratch to fit inside it. This was an amazing achievement considering that it was a listed building under the protection of English Heritage. For those readers who are not familiar with it, half of the building had to be retained or even restored to original Odeon styling but the back half of the building – where 'The Round' is located – was permitted this drastic treatment. At this point I was starting to feel the physical strain of doing manual work and regular 'ghosts'[12], so I wanted to find a better solution to rickety old stepladders for access to the lighting rig in the new venue. That's when I developed the idea of using the tension wire 'trampoline' mesh mentioned earlier. I

---

[12] 'Ghost' means all night work.

asked Kath how it had changed her life style compared to the old days at the much loved but poorly equipped Westwood.

"Technically speaking, there is nothing at Westwood that I would go back to! Westwood was a wonderful place, but it was all to do with personalities and atmosphere."

Most directors and actors that have experienced it would probably make similar comments. In Kath's opinion, the main benefits at Westborough are without doubt the mesh system and the dimmer distribution.

The mesh saves an incredible amount of time and energy, allows electrics and stage crews to work simultaneously in safety, and allows very fast turn-arounds because the colours are so easily accessible. The distribution of 240 dimmers means there is no more repatching during a show, and in a good season, between shows in the repertoire. Amazingly, no-one has had to work right through the night since the mesh was installed – something that visiting technical crews do not believe until they get there.

A typical fit up for Kath and her crew would involve a 10am to 7pm Sunday re-rig followed by 'refreshments' and an early night for a fresh start to focusing on Monday morning. Kath appreciates the benefits of having a crew who are not over-tired during the fit-up week.

If things do start to get a bit behind schedule, it is possible to have four crew members all focusing at once because of the ease of access. This is not strictly true of specials because the lighting designer can only really deal with one at a time, but for the general cover and scroller wash, all the crew should know the standard focus and be able to get on with it unsupervised.

I was very glad to hear Kath so enthusiastic about the mesh, but as it had caused some controversy in the industry when it was first installed, I was interested to hear if it had any drawbacks.

One of the good things about the system is that it allows instruments to be rigged virtually anywhere. However, this available flexibility can encourage relatively large rigs, which in itself is not a problem but when the access is gained by walking through the rig, care has to be taken not to knock things out of focus. As much of the equipment is still quite new, it is very easy to accidentally rotate a barndoor that might otherwise be held fairly solidly in older and bent lanterns.

Another potential problem is that of shadows of the mesh. The closer the lenses are to the mesh, the less likely this is, so smaller equipment may need extra long hook clamps. There will always be a shadow of some sort, but it should be so far out of focus that it is not visible to the audience. When Kath and her crew first started to experiment with lighting through the mesh, they got a nasty shock when they could clearly see the mesh shadow on the floor from behind the lantern. In fact, this is to do with the viewing angle and the shadow can be seen by the technician doing the focusing, but not by the lighting designer at floor level or the audience.

The shadow also becomes more obvious when movement is introduced; either by the focus crew walking around on the mesh, or by a moving effect such as an animation disk or effects projection. This is only really noticeable to the technical crew who know what it is they are seeing rather than to ordinary audience members who will see it only as part of the general break up projection. A shadow that cannot be lost occurs when lighting to the top of the stairs, due to the combination of throw and angle (see *Figure 19*). Remember lying in bed making shadow animals on the wall? The closer your hands are to the wall, the clearer the image. When you light through the mesh to the top of the stairs, the mesh shadow is rather too clearly cast onto the curtains at the back of the auditorium.

Kath summarises by concluding that the benefits of a physically easy rig and a well rested crew far outweigh any drawback caused by a small amount of shadow. The mesh allows the crew suitable comfort and produces a safe working environment.

As Kath is so pleased with the technical advances of the new Westborough building, I questioned what she would change if she were in a position to design the lighting facilities for that venue again. There were two main points. She would change the dimmer distribution slightly; they are evenly spaced throughout the whole grid whereas she would concentrate a greater cluster in the centre. Secondly she would change the bar layout slightly. With hindsight it is obvious but at the time, a bar layout was drawn up and then rigs designed to fit this layout. What should have been done was to design the 'ideal general cover' and then mark the desired bar positions on the plan around the rig. It's not so obvious to work that way at the time because you are conditioned through old working practices to design a rig around the available rigging points and not vice versa.

On the subject of disadvantages to lighting theatre-in-the-round as opposed to proscenium or end stage productions, Kath does miss the ability to 'close down' on a scene, particularly after a big musical number. It can be done with specials if the cast members are static at the right time, but what is occasionally called for is follow spots which are rarely a viable option in this staging format because of the risk of spilling into the auditorium. Kath had a battle with one guest director on this issue but she eventually won her case, if only on the grounds of there not being enough crew members available! Thinking back, the only time I saw followspots used was in 1988 in a production of *The Ballroom* by Peter King. It was very tricky and the only way it worked was by choreographing the dance around where the spots could safely reach to – something that ordinary choreographers and dancers in ordinary venues would never tolerate!

Of the examples that I have mentioned in this book, the reader may have noticed two or three shows being mentioned several times. This is because I have a particular fondness of those in addition to the fact that they provided the examples I needed. Kath also has her own favourite shows, and one that came immediately to her mind was *Perfect Pitch* which is set on a camping site from dusk 'til dawn. I was pleased with her selection when she started to describe it because she had achieved the subtlety and visibility required of prolonged night scenes in what sounded like a very similar style to the way that I tackled *Dreams From A Summerhouse*. Her choice of moonlight colours was very similar: Supergel #68 (sky blue) and Lee 200 (double CT blue) contrasted with #007 (pale yellow) and 205 (½ CT orange), along with all those 10 and 20 minute fades. While we were discussing colour, she spotted my quote from Stephen Joseph:

> "It is not usual to fit colour filters to spotlights to the extent that is common practice for proscenium stage work ... of course colour may be used... but the main scheme will not depend upon it."

and laughed explaining that: "Colour is one of the most exciting things about lighting theatre-in-the-round."

In this we both agree, and beg to differ from the guru himself.

David Taylor, Lighting Designer and Theatre Consultant

I am happy to be able to include some contributions from David Taylor in this book because of his varied experiences in theatre lighting. I am hoping, David the designer and David the consultant would offer contradictory opinions about designing show lighting and designing venue lighting expressed in this chapter!

Photograph 25: David Taylor at work in the TPC office in Connecticut.

The shows that David described to me were performed in a variety of theatres including the New Orange Tree Theatre in London, The Drum at Plymouth Theatre Royal and the Embassy Studio, London. Each of the venues have their own specific logistical problems, and their lighting grid designs are all quite different. From a first glance of the plans, the Drum looks by far the most difficult venue to work in as there are only two catwalks over the stage area and the rest of the lighting positions are all around the perimeter. However, as David's photographs of *Animal Island* show, this apparent lack of rigging positions is not at all limiting to the lighting designer's art.

Animal Island is a children's musical and therefore a fantasy production full of theatrical tricks such as a fully rigged pirate ship and a practical volcano. David Taylor took the 'bash-it-in' approach to lighting this production: strong sources, strong colours and strong angles. His rig included a surprising quantity of 2kW profiles and Parcans, and utilised Reich and Vogel beamlights as followspots. The profiles focused across the stage and Parcans rigged as downlights were used to create 'walls of light' which had the ability both to open up the stage and close down on specific areas. Had they been around at the time, David suggested that digital light curtains would have done this job beautifully. The walls of light were in saturated colours and the beamlights cut through these in high contrast, allowing the main characters to be set apart from the background. Effects projectors were also used to enhance the smoke effects and to give a 'sea-like experience'.

In the same venue, David also lit *Entertaining Mr. Sloane*. Ordinarily a more naturalistic style would be expected, but the 'rubbish tip' set design allowed a more stylised approach to the lighting. Parts of the set extended into the balcony, thus greying the stage/audience divide in a similar fashion to the pub booths in the Scarborough production of *Conversations With My Father*. The items around the stage perimeter of the Entertaining Mr. Sloane set included 'lightable' objects such as car headlights and an old fridge providing good set dressing potential.

Photograph 26: 'Animal Island' at the Drum Theatre.
Photograph: David Taylor

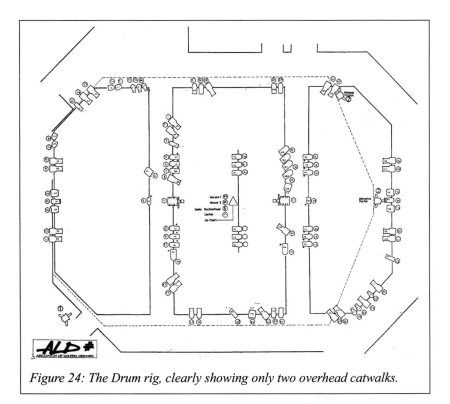

Figure 24: The Drum rig, clearly showing only two overhead catwalks.

A strong vertical practical cover in the centre of the stage resulted in two different and distinctive lighting styles within the one production. The choice of colours – a mix of warm colour correction and a mauve tint – created a suitably 'seedy' feel to the general lighting scenes. At the Orange Tree Theatre, of favourite shows David talks of Sam Walters' production of the restoration comedy *All In The Wrong*. The design had a warm creamy feel to it, reflected in the set, costumes and lighting all working together. The Orange Tree rig is, like The New Vic, comprised predominantly of profiles. For *All In The Wrong*, David needed to soften the impact of these instruments without resorting to the use of frost (Frosting will not help you keep stray light off the audience when focusing…). The colour palette was based around warm and cool colour correction filters, plus Rosco skyblue for the night scenes. Parcans were also used as three-quarter backlight to add some dimensionality to the pictures, but the positioning of these was determined as much by the uncontrollable spill that they cause as by the desired effect itself. These were, of course, the days before Blackwrap!

On the subject of frost, from his comments, David clearly dislikes this method of lighting in all staging formats, saying that:

> *"Lighting design should be about light arriving at the subject, not wallying around in the lens and colour carrier of the instrument."*

Since *All In The Wrong*, he has seen several shows at the Orange Tree where frosting the whole rig has become a common occurrence. At Scarborough, with my general rig of Fresnels I was never faced with this problem although when I first 'inherited' the rig, frosted Pattern 23s were used as vom frontlight. I found these quite unsatisfactory because they were not wide enough and there was always a visible line between the general area lighting and the vom lighting, so I soon got into the habit of using PCs instead. But the Orange Tree is not the only theatre-in-the-round with a basic rig of profiles – there's Jo Dawson at The New Vic with her Preludes and 264s, and my experience of Cantatas and Cadenzas at the Cottesloe. Neither venues need to resort to using frost as the luminaires can be focused soft enough to blend with Fresnels and to allow specials to cut through them. So once I'd dispensed with my unsatisfactory vom lighting, I only used frost in very specific specials: a light Hamburg for pinspots or, on one occasion, a silk in order to stretch the beam of a prelude in one direction to compensate for the necessity of it being rigged at a particularly short throw to the tall set piece that it was lighting.

David enjoys the theatre-in-the-round staging format because of the way that the audience becomes an integral part of the performance and indeed, the venue. He feels that a proscenium can actually handicap a strong piece of theatre because of the divide between stage and audience that it creates. As a potential drawback of our favoured staging format, he comments on the cut off angle when focusing towards the auditorium *(Figures 4 and 18)* and how difficult this can be due to "actors yearning to sit in the laps of the audience".

The only successful way to light actors on the edge of the stage is if there is a clearly defined 'no-go' zone between stage an auditorium – which is a slight contradiction of the concept of the audience being a part of the production. In Scarborough this slight separation is achieved naturally by a low step up to the front row. The most difficult venues to work in

Photograph 27: 'All In the Wrong' at The Orange Tree.
Lighting Design and photograph: David I Taylor

are those where the stage and the front row are on the same level because there is no deliniation between these two areas.

He has tried various methods of creating distinctive side and back light around the edges of arena stages, but recognises the dangers of creating an unwanted 'wall' rather than a free and open feeling. Finding the right balance between lively, dimensional lighting and keeping a suitable separation from the audience is a problem that is different in every venue and every lighting designer will establish their own method for achieving this.

For colour washes, David has often managed multiple colours by adding a second 90 or 120 degree cover at a similar degree of rotation form the main cover, although since his earlier experiences of theatre-in-the-round he can see the advantages in using scrollers or colour-faders. He has not used moving lights for drama because of their lack of subtlety, but is looking forward to a new generation of instruments where colour and gobo 'morphing' will be more readily available. He has had more success with the use of followspots, most notably the Reich & Vogels on *Animal Island*. He says that the best position to rig them is in the corners of a rectangular space, but obviously the available rigging points and effectiveness are venue-specific. Great care has to be taken by the followspot operators to avoid bounce and glare into the audience. Ideally, David hypothesises, there should be more followspots in a theatre-in-the-round production than in an end-stage venue to ensure that all sides of the audience benefit from equal amounts of front and back light. However, as this staging format is often in small and under-funded venues, show budgets will often prevent this requirement. Personally, I would rather not use them at all than to use them inefficiently or badly.

As well as lighting a show at the Orange Tree, David was involved in its development, along with Iain Mackintosh, in his role of Theatre Consultant for Theatre Projects Consultants. Generally he is very pleased with the facilities at the Orange Tree, although he would like to see more dimmers and move the houselights to a less obtrusive position. The venue is in many ways similar to Scarborough Westwood: similar stage dimensions and a fixed grid based on approximately 1.2m centres – just enough space for three instrument side by side within the same grid section. The rig consists mainly of Cantata profiles with a few Fresnels, but there is also a good stock of smaller equipment that is physically able to squeeze into those awkward spaces. Additionally, there are ladders dropped below the main grid level to provide some good low-level positions. The size, shape and grid layout of this venue support the use of a 120 degree general cover well.

Strangely, considering his fondness for the Orange Tree, with his consultant hat on David prefers the catwalk method for grid access in a new theatre-in-the-round. If he were to develop a formula for designing a grid, would draw up what could be considered the 'optimum' number of catwalks, and then remove one of them to open up some free space. This method prevents one of my 'catwalk-fears' that there is more structure than lighting positions. If it is that important to rig an instrument in the space created by the 'missing catwalk' then temporary scaffolding can be rigged on a show-by-show basis. The catwalks provide a safe and easy working environment for personnel of all abilities and levels of experience, and create a passive visual ceiling to the space. Curiously they are the very same arguments that I would put forward in favour of the wire mesh grid.

David conceded that he might specify such a structure in a venue staffed by established professionals as it allows enormous flexibility to the *"qualified and safe user"*. Here we seem to have a slight difference of

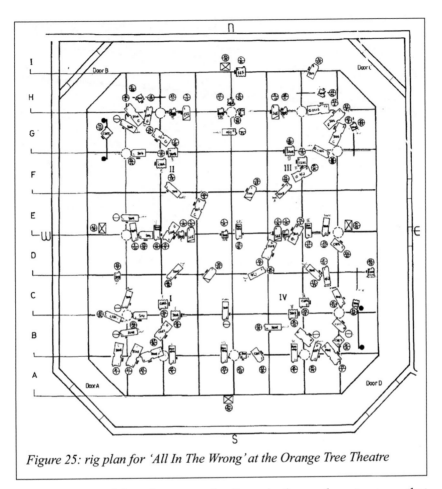

Figure 25: rig plan for 'All In The Wrong' at the Orange Tree Theatre

opinion as one of the advantages that I saw in the mesh system was that it is inherently safe for all users – you can't fall off of it, and you can't drop heavy objects to floor.

One of the most notable TPC theatre-in-the-round projects is Manchester's Royal Exchange Theatre, both pre- and post-IRA bomb rebuild in 1998. The Theatre Projects philosophy is *"to make the most dimensional and effective environment for the creating of theatre performance"* and that philosophy was applied to the Royal Exchange.

One of the facilities added to the venue during the rebuild is a major Ethernet network to allow the lighting control position to be located anywhere in the

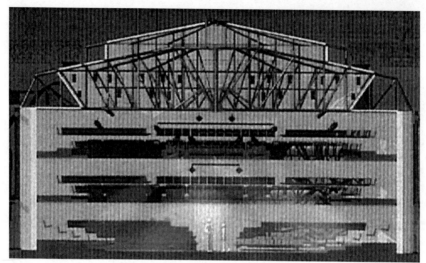

Figure 26: Section through the Royal Exchange Theatre.

auditorium, as well as providing effective distribution for all DMX devices such as moving lights and scrollers. The quantity of dimmers has been massively increased – from 180 to 400 – via a hard patch to over 1,200 socket outlets. Surely they will never need to use an extension cable again!

Attention has been paid to keeping services discrete and there are cunning 'cheese box' panels built into the curves of the auditorium to provide – and hide – lighting and sound outlets.

The refurbishment budget allowed for the purchase of 14 moving lights to be permanently rigged on the 'spokes' of the module, providing general purpose moving light facilities and therefore reducing the annual lighting hire bill.

The most important of these additional facilities seems to be the increase in dimmers and sockets – at last theatre-in-the-round is seen as being resource heavy, instead of the mythical cheap alternative performance space that it is so often perceived to be.

Jo Dawson, Chief Electrician and Lighting Designer New Vic Theatre, Newcastle-Under-Lyme

Jo Dawson worked at the New Vic Theatre (formally The New Victoria) for around ten years, latterly as Chief Electrician and Lighting Designer.

Although the New Vic regularly uses freelance lighting designers, Jo lit most productions there in her last three years there. I asked her for her cooperation with this book so as to present some fresh opinions (after all, Mick Hughes and Kath Geraghty have both worked with me at Scarborough), but also to provide a few more non Scarborough design examples.

Photograph 28: Jo Dawson in the electrician's office at the New Vic Theatre. Photograph: Jackie Staines

Although the stage at the New Vic Theatre is considerably larger than Scarborough or Bowness, (10 x 9m and 7.6m high) the general cover is still divided into a basic nine areas plus entrances. The nine area method seems to have been well tried and tested in all of the venues discussed in this book apart from The Rose Theatre with its 13 areas. Nine areas work well at the New Vic because the grid is considerably higher than the other purpose-built round venues, so there is extra throw to allow light beams to cover the stage from this height. Jo has stuck to using four sided cover although some guest designers have tried using the 120° rule, although not particularly successfully in the New Vic. Unlike the other venues discussed, the rig at Newcastle-Under-Lyme consists mainly of profiles, and the general cover is achieved by using 650W profiles. For most shows, there is a single colour in the general cover but it is common to add a scroller wash that will give a versatile choice of 'all purpose' colours, and if these are rigged on Parcans or 2kW Fresnels, some very punchy effects can be achieved. Unfortunately where Kath only has 12 scrollers, Jo is only marginally better off with 14. Both venues would benefit from doubling their quantity of these devices.

Generally Jo is quite happy with her assortment of equipment which consists mainly of profiles and Parcans and only 20 Fresnels – unlike Scarborough and Bowness where the opposite is true. I would tend to suggest that a general cover by profiles is not ideal, but in many ways it is more versatile as it allows for gobos and shuttering everywhere. I'm glad to have discovered this contradiction of general cover methods. Along with the Parcan cover at Rose Bruford College, they show that any equipment can be used and it is up to the individual designers and technicians to make the available equipment work in the most effective way, and up to the reader to decide which approach they would prefer if faced with the choice.

Access to the lighting instruments in the New Vic is by catwalks and during my conversation with Jo, I was pleasantly surprised to find they are extremely well designed with easy and comfortable rigging positions, and there are a lot more available rigging points than I imagined. Personally I think that I would miss the versatility of the Scarborough grids although Jo told me that rarely is there a desire or need to rig in impossible places, and with a selection of varied length hook clamps, she is able to poke lens tubes right underneath the catwalks when necessary. However, in a similar fashion to the sketches in Chapter 1, Jo told me that the centre area of her grid has a tendency to become very crowded, intensified by the large gap in the centre of the catwalk design. The catwalks appear to be suspended from the roof structure, but are in fact perfectly rigid and stable to walk on. This fixed access allows several technicians to work simultaneously in comfort and safety, although Jo

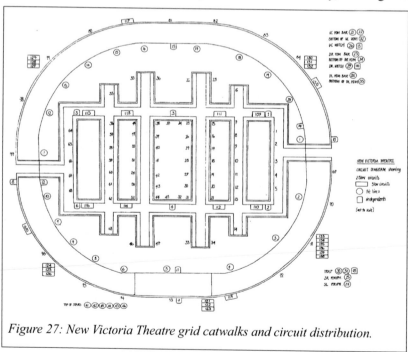

Figure 27: New Victoria Theatre grid catwalks and circuit distribution.

would like to see the installation of another set of steps to the grid as the existing two can become congested during rigging and focusing.

This grid allows neat and convenient storage for instruments not in use. They can either remain in the grid itself or be stored on the numerous bars and spaces around the perimeters of the 'service' gallery level. Jo and her crew seem to have very disciplined housekeeping habits as the whole area was neat, tidy and well organised as I seem to remember it was on a previous visit I made to the New Vic a few years ago. It all makes for a very pleasant working environment.

The only obvious drawback of the New Vic grid design is the lack of circuits. There are currently 138 dimmer circuits and Jo would like to see this increased to at least 200. She couldn't believe the New Stephen Joseph Theatre is equipped with 240, and found the concept of managing on 60 dimmers in the old venue even more bemusing!

Beneath the main grid of catwalks at the New Vic Theatre are two 'gallery bars' which give the opportunity of using some very shallow angles in what otherwise seems to be quite a steep grid providing a fairly consistent beam angle into all acting areas. Jo favours these gallery angles for colour and gobo washes, and it is a feature that she thinks she will miss when she takes the New Vic production of *The Mikado* to Scarborough.

Having experienced many occasions where the voms have been important acting and therefore lighting areas, I asked Jo what method she used for lighting into these positions. She told me that this is quite a recent phenomena because in the days of Peter Cheeseman's directorship, there was a clear distinction between 'on' and 'off' stage and these areas were not used by the performers for 'acting', only as the 'route' to and from the acting area. It was therefore not deemed necessary to devise a method of successfully lighting these areas. More recently, since the appointment of Gwenda Hughes as artistic director, there is more frequent use of these areas so they are now often lit steeply from the grid to the front and from inside the vom tunnels for backlight. This is an interesting point for anyone designing a new theatre-in-the-round auditorium: provision needs to be made for vom backlighting both in terms of dimmer distribution and for physical rigging positions, bearing in mind that these areas often have limited head height in many venues.

I failed to coax Jo into owning up to any technical disasters or difficulties, although she did mention getting badly behind schedule when focusing

Littlevoice because it was a very large rig requiring very precise focusing. Also *Second To Last In The Sack Race* was onstage at the time of my visit.

The set was a model village complete with illuminating buildings and a model railway! To cope with the cabling requirements, the stage floor was raised a few inches to provide cable routes and extra circuits were dropped down from the grid by a multicore to provide the necessary distribution. More interestingly, although there were no other New Vic shows in repertoire at the time, the stage did have bookings for outside events during the run so all the buildings were designed to simply plug in to the under floor cabling to enable fast and safe removal and replacement of the set. The production of *The Wizard of Oz* posed a lighting problem – the hurricane – although it was solved artistically rather than technically. The solution was to use a rotating gobo centre stage as a point of focus, but to run a chase sequence around audience lighting to give a greater impression of fast movement.

As with every venue that an individual works in for a long period of time, there are certain 'methods' that work for lighting in specific styles and Jo will sometimes use these tried and tested methods. For example, the gallery bars with their relatively flat angles are good for atmospheric gobo washes.

Although the lights from this angle will cover the whole of the stage *floor*, they will not cover it at head height. Such a gobo wash must be supplemented from the main grid to achieve the required cover, but *appears* only to be coming from the gallery bar. This is Jo's equivalent to my 'cross-washes' discussed earlier.

Jo seemed very content with her lot at the New Vic; she is happy with the grid, the desk, would like a few more dimmers, and obviously gets a great sense of artistic fulfilment from her work. Is this venue really so perfect? I put the hypothetical question and asked what she would do with a financial gift that was to be used specifically for improving the lighting facilities. Her somewhat modest answer was to replace some of her gobo projecting stock for newer profiles. I say modest because she stated *some* rather than *all*. Was she looking a proverbial gift horse in the mouth? Her answer was very reasoned – she wanted to ditch some of her older stock, specifically the 264s, for something that would give sharper gobo images for specific specials, but she also likes the 'soft' quality of subtle gobo washes that she might lose if she upgraded the whole rig with new, bright, sharp luminaires.

We discussed her choice of preferred luminaire to improve her luminaire stock and she thought she would probably chose Strand SLs. She did not opt for ETC Source Fours because she felt that they have a very distinctive beam quality which is normally a good thing, but felt that these instruments would not blend well with the rest of her equipment and that the SLs would suit the venue better. After a hint she asked for some more scrollers too, but the general impression she gave me was one of fond contentment for her job, her theatre and its equipment.

Unlike the other venues discussed, the New Vic Theatre does have follow spots permanently installed. They tend to remain in set positions, not because of lack of imagination or enthusiasm, but because of physical restrictions within the upper gallery level. The followspots have been used on numerous occasions and with some careful choreography of swapping the spots over to light the performer on the opposite side, they are generally successful. This could well be because of the extra height allowing steeper followspot angles, but also because the house policy is to be reasonably lenient towards occasional light spillage into the audience during these types of shows. Jo is using followspots on *The Mikado* and while I was there, she received the disappointing news that this will not be possible when the show transfers to Scarborough.

Asked to describe some of the differences and pros and cons of theatre-in-the-round over proscenium and end stage formats, her immediate answer was the intimacy of theatre-in-the-round compared to the somewhat false detachment between actors and audience in proscenium theatre. The proscenium creates a kind of 'us and them' feeling between performer and spectator which is quite unnatural. Jo compared this to watching television, where the viewer is looking at a small object a long way away. Theatre-in-the-round is far more natural because the very nature of proscenium theatre is that the shape of the stage dictates the blocking.

She enjoys the creativity of theatre-in-the-round and the fact that the lighting designer sometimes has to do the work that a set designer would normally do in other staging formats, and that the atmosphere and location of the piece is entirely dependent upon lighting and sound. It is unusual in other staging formats to use the floor as a canvas in the way that it is often necessary in theatre-in-the-round. I put to Jo the argument that theatre-in-the-round can be flat, boring, textureless, colourless and bland (as argued by some non theatre-in-the-round lighting designers!). She immediately contradicted this opinion by explaining that the opposite is true and lighting theatre-in-the-round actually relies on textures and shapes and colour. As she says: "What makes light interesting is the absence of it," and she doesn't find the theatre-in-the-round staging format at all limiting to the lighting designer or their ideas and commented that it is: "A really wonderful way to light theatre."

Jo enjoys the opportunity of making bold statements across the stage, as *Photograph 30* of the New Vic production of *Oliver Twist* shows. It confirms that Jo has a bold streak to her designs, but what about her opinions on backlight and keylight in theatre-in-the-round? There was a long pause preceding her answer to the "What is backlight" question. Then she began by saying: "I think it exists, but only for some of the audience". She feels that the very nature of theatre-in-the-round is that it looks different from every audience position and that the audience must accept that as the nature of the beast; if it all looked the same, it would

Photograph 30: 'Oliver Twist' at the New Vic Theatre. Lighting: Jo Dawson, Set and photography: Sue Condie.

be terribly boring. As backlight to 70% of the audience is by definition frontlight to the remaining 30%, there is therefore no 'true' backlight, apart possibly from that emanating from the voms. A similar answer to Kath Geraghty at Scarborough who stated that every backlight is someone else's front light and that dramatic backlight tableaux can only be used for short scenes or dramatic statements.

Jo went on to emphasise the importance of keylight in theatre-in-the-round as it is what immediately portrays the picture, location and time. Although it can come from any direction, Jo doesn't feel as strongly as I do over the importance of trying to change the direction of the keylight. After all, if the windows are on one side of the stage they have to stay there, although it is possible to vary the angle of light through the window during the course of the play.

Where I discussed *Dreams From A Summerhouse* earlier in this book and Kath mentioned *Perfect Pitch*, Jo described a similar approach to the problem of lighting a scene of prolonged darkness. She would start by choosing the base dark blue, because it suggests night-time to the audience. This is likely to be something like Lee 143 (pale navy blue) or even double 143 for naturalistic scenes or a deeper primary blue for more stylised productions. On top of this, she will add a wash of break-up gobos in a dark blue and if required, moonlight. For the moonlight she would most likely use Lee 161 (slate blue) – a technique picked up from Paul Jones who lit a lot of shows at the New Victoria before Jo and during her earlier years there. I was amused that they both chose my own favoured moonlight colour. I explained that during my conversation with Kath Geraghty, she had used a very similar approach on *Perfect Pitch*, and as the show had transferred to the New Vic, I asked Jo for her opinion on the lighting. She agreed that the colour scheme was quite similar to what she might have done herself, but felt that it was plotted a lot brighter than her preference. (When I asked Kath about transferring the show, she complained that the general cover at the New Vic was too dark!). Jo went on to explain that Peter Cheeseman had encouraged dark and atmospheric lighting and that she generally found visiting shows quite bright and it was therefore not a specific criticism of *Perfect Pitch* but an overall observation between the work of the New Vic and the work of other theatre-in-the-round companies.

Considering this exchange of opinion over the balance of the general cover illumination at Stoke and Scarborough, and considering that Jo and Kath have both transferred shows to each other's venues, I asked Jo to explain some of the differences between the venues and problems that she was anticipating for her transfer of *The Mikado*, during the summer of 2000.

Her main concern was of the discrepancy between the general cover of the two venues: the 1.2kW Fresnels at Scarborough are twice the power of her own Prelude general cover and she was seriously contemplating asking Kath to exchange them for 650W PCs. Perhaps they will reach a compromise with a few sheets of neutral density...

Jo will also miss her low-level gallery positions and the use of follow-spots that *The Mikado* requires and she is contemplating taking some extra Parcans for colour washes, but otherwise she is quite happy with the Scarborough venue.

She explained that she had been pleasantly surprised the first time she saw the wire mesh grid. It did not absorb as much light as she expected and the holes in the mesh are much larger than she anticipated (3" squares). From what she had heard, she was expecting a mesh more like that of chicken wire but in reality there are far more holes than solid wire. Some of the access is not particularly good because of the positions of roof structures and air-conditioning ducts and she was surprised that it had been 'designed' that way. However, Jo was not at that time aware of the structural constraints and limitations caused by putting this system into an existing building shell rather than designing the roof void from scratch – because the building is listed, the roof profile had to remain in its original stepped shape and could not be raised to an even level across its whole span.

She was not at all perturbed by seeing pools of light on the mesh because the audience is used to seeing the lights up there anyway, and once a show begins the audience rarely look up into the grid. In fact, many flying pieces of set have escaped the notice of an audience altogether because they are so focused on the stage and the actors! Jo used four Martin MAC 250s on a rock & roll musical recently and was quite pleased with the result. The budget only allowed for two larger fixtures or four 250s, so she traded brightness for quantity. As they were cutting over a general rig of 650W Preludes they balanced well any way but as Jo said, it's not the intensity but the movement that gets noticed. She rigged them two either side of the centre line across the horizontal centre line on the rig plan shown in *Figure 27 on page 30* and from these positions she was able to cover the whole stage area with bright colour washes. She preferred these to moving mirror fixtures as she found the range of movement of the mirrors too restricted for that venue.

Jo's lighting style again shows the importance of a good general cover but also how lighting theatre-in-the-round can be pushed to limits of imagination, daring, budget and technical resources.

7 REMEMBRANCE

Just as I began this book by acknowledging the life and work of Stephen Joseph, the credited founder of theatre-in-the-round in Britain, it seems fitting to end it on a note of remembrance for the man who brought new theories and ideas to the performing arts and provided me personally and many other people with the opportunity of working in what is a very rewarding and inventive theatre format. The transcript below of Stephen Joseph's memorial service address is followed by his obituary as published in TABS.

This is not an occasion for sorrow, but rather one of joy. Joy that a man has passed through our midst, touching our lives at various points, leaving each one of us the richer for his passage.

Stephen has given us so much from the wealth that he discovered in life that there can be no-one who came into contact with him who did not receive some fresh revelation, some surprising insight, some flash of inspiration which will have thrown new light on their problems, their work, their hobbies, or on the humblest of their daily tasks. I suppose that each one of us has tried to discover the particular secret that made Stephen so different from the majority of men we meet. What was the key to his unbound enthusiasm? What made us so anxious to share his company, and share his views even when we disagreed with him? I believe that it was a very simple secret – it was his ability to look on the world and all that happens in it as something that is happening for the first time, as a discovery that must be made by each one of us, as if it had never been seen or felt before, as a challenge which demands the full use of the faculties which God has given us. Not that he denied the wisdom and experience of others, but that he believed in man's right to question, to probe for the truth, to discover for himself. Life was for Stephen Joseph an adventure, a challenge, a question and an endless wonder. He met it with the eyes of a child and the mind of a man. Eyes that saw everything as if for the first time, unblurred by the preconceptions of tradition and a mind that he had trained to distinguish between truth and falsehood, emotion and sentiment and, above all, between beauty and its many imitations.

For Stephen, beauty lay in the way a man works, as well as in the completed work itself. He taught us to endow each work we undertake – however humble – with the care and love of a craftsman. It is as a craftsman that many of us will remember him – as a man who worked with his hands as well as his head. For him there was no such thing as a menial task – the skill of the stagehand was equal to the skill of the playwright. Workmanship was the basic of all art. If he was a perfectionist it was as a lover of a simple task well done, rather than ambition to create a masterpiece or become a public figure. For Stephen, beauty was to be found in all humble things – even more perhaps than in the complexities of creation. The beauty of a leaf, of a kitten at play, the beauty of carpentry, the beauty of and old-world melodrama or an early film. It was, I think, this love of simple craftsmanship that led him to champion the course that will ever be associated with his name – theatre-in-the-round. He was drawn to this form of theatre – not that he despised other more elaborate forms – for a variety of reasons. He saw it as a challenge to the outworn conventions of a theatre that was rapidly losing touch with humanity. He saw it as a stimulus to a new approach by actors and playwrights as an opportunity to create more vital relationships between actors and audience, but above all he saw in theatre-in-the-round the simplest form of dramatic performance, springing from the earliest days of man's history when poet, actor, and artist were united as craftsmen. This unity of man's God-given faculties – the unity of head, heart and hands – is the quality that Stephen championed, it is the challenge that he holds out to those of us who have loved and admired him. This love of simple things, this pride in our work however humble, this perpetual discovery of life for ourselves, this never-ending search for truth – these are the secrets Stephen discovered, the riches that he leaves behind. Stephen is not dead as long as we preserve these things. He lives on, in us and with us.
October 1967

Stephen Joseph whose death at the age of forty-six was announced last month, will be sadly missed by all who knew him and not least by those who had met him in his articles in the pages of TABS or in the many books of his we reviewed from time to time. His writing style was very like the man himself, a stimulating director and teacher boiling over with enthusiasm, but all the time one was conscious that here was an expert who really knew his subject.

*Literature and acting were literally in Stephen's blood and he studied widely spending much time in the United States. He was a trained scene designer which came as something of a surprise due to his apparent espousal to a theatre with no scenery. His spirit of adventure got him the D.S.O. with his command in the R.N.V.R. during World War II and got him into battles of another kind afterwards. He was **the expert** on how to start and run theatre on the slenderest of financial and physical resources. This made his writings helpful to a very wide circle indeed. The booklet he wrote at our request in 1962 was a very typical example of his lively style and of the economy of means suggested to practice what he preached.*

Stephen Joseph founded the successful Victoria Theatre, Stoke on Trent (a neat conversion by him of a cinema into a theatre-in-the-round of 345 seats) [now the New Victoria Theatre – J.S.] and although managerial dissent featured in the press a while back we should remember that Stephen was by then a very sick man indeed – an active man caged by his bed. What his friends, and he had so many, would like to remember him by would be a permanent theatre for his Studio Company in Scarborough. The tours of this company and the many annual summer seasons in the ingeniously converted but cramped quarters of the library in Scarborough were most characteristic of this enthusiastic pioneer. A 'Stephen Joseph' theatre, in the round, in that town would be a true and deserved memorial.

TABS Editor
November 1967

Stephen Joseph: 1921 - 1967

A1 PLANNING FOR NEW THEATRE FORMS

The following nine pages, which include the chapters 'Lighting-in-the-Round' and 'Production-in-the-Round' are reproduced with kind permission of Strand Lighting Ltd. directly from *Planning New Forms Of Theatre* by Stephen Joseph (revised and enlarged third edition) published by The Strand Electric and Engineering Co. Ltd in 1966.

LIGHTING-IN-THE-ROUND

To eke out the meagre help given by the examples above, let us go into a bit more detail with at least one theatre, under more or less ideal conditions, but keeping within the sober bounds of possibility. I choose a theatre-in-the-round for two reasons. Firstly because I know more about this than the other new forms. And secondly because it is the extreme form as far as the embrace of the audience is concerned.

A theatre-in-the-round intended for use as a professional play-house can be served by a capacity between 250 and 400, and these will be the limits taken for granted here unless otherwise indicated. In the Victoria Theatre, Stoke-on-Trent, for example, 350 people are accommodated in five or six rows (Fig. 23).

The acting area will be about 18 ft. by 24 ft., and this may be taken as an optimum size. A bigger acting area will begin to destroy one of the characteristics of this form of theatre –the close physical proximity of audience to actors. The same seems likely to apply to other forms of open stage, and a reasonable criticism of the Festival Theatre in Chichester is that the acting area is too big.

In section across stage and auditorium the acting area should be at the lowest level, and the five rows of seats must be raised in steps (Fig. 24).

If possible, I would like to have one or two balconies, each with a single row of seats and behind it special accommodation for standing. In this way a theatre with a capacity of a thousand could be built with no one more than 20 ft. from the acting area. It is stimulating to actors to have the audience spread up the walls, closely packed, and as close as possible.

We can now examine the specific business of lighting the stage.

Firstly, stage lighting for all forms of open stage will come from spotlights. Floodlights and battens have virtually no application and will not be further mentioned. The most suitable lantern is a soft edge spotlight with a fresnel lens and a beam that can be adjusted within the approximate limits of 15° to 45°, and using a 500-watt lamp.

Profile spots and other lanterns and lamps may also be useful, and some attention will be drawn to them when they might be preferred. But the general scheme can be most simply described by restricting reference to one sort of lantern. Note that the Strand Pattern 264 uses a 1,000-watt lamp and has adjustable hard/soft edges, very useful for all open stage work, though it is likely to remain more expensive than the ordinary soft edge lantern.

When positioning the spotlights ensure that in elevation the angle between the horizontal and the light beam is about 45° (see Fig. 25). If it is much more than 50° awkward shadows begin to be

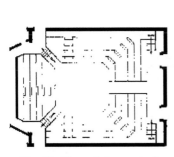

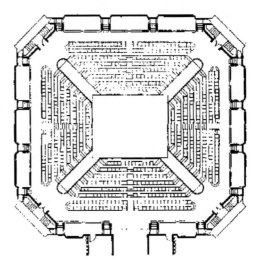

Fig. 23. *Plans of theatres-in-the-round drawn to same scale. Left: Victoria, Stoke-on-Trent. Right: the overlarge Arena, Washington, D.C.*

formed, particularly round the actors' eyes. Note that this applies in any form of theatre, but don't forget that it may be an effect positively required on special occasions. The angle can be less than 45°, but if it is much less than 25° difficulty may be experienced in keeping direct light out of the eyes of the audience. The beam angle required will mean that a substantial proportion of the spotlights are positioned not so much over the acting area as over the seating rows—and probably towards the outer walls of the auditorium. When arranging positions for spotlights, remember that the light should cover the actors and in elevational drawings it is worth taking a line about 5 ft. 6 in. above the acting area level and ensuring that beam angles spread along this line. Similarly, when adjusting the spotlights for lighting a play, the producer will ensure that

Fig. 24. *Section through a theatre-in-the-round of about 350 capacity in 5 rows. Acting area at lowest level, first row raised 6 in., other rows rising by 1 ft. each. Seating levels are 3 ft. deep.*

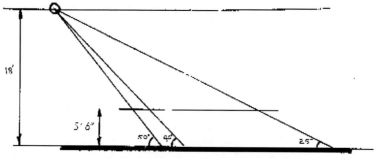

FIG. 25. *Section showing critical lighting angles.*

actors' faces are lit though he may be misled by the patterns of light on the floor itself.

It is not usual to fit colour filters to spotlights to the extent that is common practice for proscenium stage work. For the latter, one of the important functions of colour is to help emphasise the solidity of three-dimensional objects (including actors). But owing to the proximity of the audience in theatre-in-the-round this is not necessary. Of course colour may be used, and for special effects it will frequently be demanded; but the main scheme will not depend on it.

The acting area is divided into separate units each of which will be lit independently but employing the same relative lantern lay-out (Fig. 26). In plan a satisfactory distribution of spotlights is achieved by having 120° separation. Alternative arrangements, such as 90° or 60° separation, are perfectly possible, with their particular advantages and snags, but 120° is recommended for simplicity, efficiency and economy and will be the only plan dealt with here. Each area unit, then, is lit by three spotlights; single spotlights are seldom used except for special effects. The plan is probably best related to the seating rows as shown, so that when area units are arranged to cover the whole acting area, advantage is taken of minimal spill (Fig. 27) into the audience. Ignoring, for the present, the many alternatives and possibilities available, but taking the factors so far recommended, a basic lighting scheme consisting of six area units can now be suggested. The lanterns should be placed in the roof void or lighting loft, the whole of which may be floored over—or walkways provided adjacent to the rows of spotlights. Handrails should be provided for safety. Spotlights can be suspended from 2 in.-diameter tube, or mounted on base plates; there are a number of possible arrangements that will both provide the necessary facilities for access to the lanterns and give the desired beam angles. Details will depend on precise design of the ceiling structure. It is worth noting that only four of the eighteen lanterns are placed directly over the acting area. This is important because it is commonly assumed that theatre-in-the-

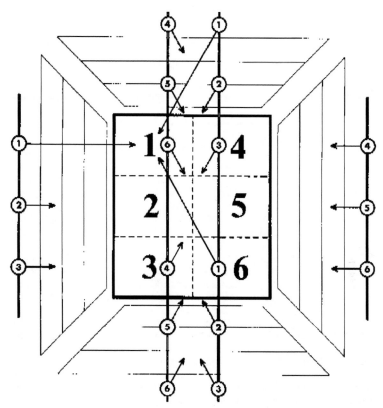

Fig. 26. *Plan showing arrangement of area units to light the stage. The acting area is divided into six sections, each of which is lit by three spotlights. The arrangement suggests four troughs in the lighting loft. (Note that only four out of the eighteen lanterns are actually over the acting area.)*

round lighting comes solely from directly over the acting area, a scheme that could provide nothing but inadequate or very peculiar illumination for the actors.

The series of unit areas so far described will enable the whole stage to be fully lit with a fairly even spread of light. Separate areas can be lit in isolation, or varying degrees of brightness given to different areas by using dimmer control (about which notes will follow). All spotlights used for lighting the unit areas will normally be set for optimum effects and left from one production to the next without any adjustment. Special effects, beyond the range of the area units, will be provided by using additional lighting

Extra lighting may be needed to cover entrances and to increase the definition of the acting area, and further lighting troughs will

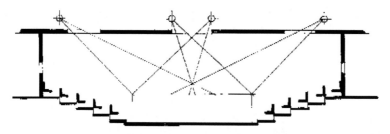

FIG. 27. *Relation of lighting and seating in section.*

probably be necessary for these purposes. Extra lighting will be required for such purposes as indicating sunlight, or daylight streaming through a window, artificial light from on-stage lamps, specially confined areas, and for colour effects. It is not possible to anticipate all the needs of a wide repertoire of plays, but a sensible calculation can be based on the provision of a dozen extra spotlights for these purposes. Use profile spotlights in each case. A diffuser glass can easily be slipped into a profile spot* to provide a soft edge when required; narrow angle or wide angle lenses can be added, and a variety of diaphragms will help to achieve all sorts of effects. Since theatre-in-the-round can handle plays in repertoire with comparative ease (not having the scenic storage problem of a proscenium theatre), this may be part of its policy as it is at the Victoria Theatre and as it was at Scarborough. Allow about six extra spotlights for each play in repertoire, up to a maximum of 30. The total number of spotlights has now reached 60. It is not anticipated that all spotlights will be used at any one time, but the control to be described will provide for easy selection.

Each spotlight position in the lighting loft should be provided with an adjacent socket outlet. However, more socket outlets than the total number of spotlights should be provided. For 60 spotlights, provide, say, 72 socket outlets and circuits. Spotlights are normally equipped with 2 ft. 6 in. tails of heat resistant cable to which plugs must be fitted. Use three-pin, 5-amp plugs and sockets throughout the system. Each socket outlet should be on cable trunking so that no loose cable need be left on the floor of the lighting loft. The trunking will lead directly into the control room where a connecting panel will provide separate flexible leads for each circuit and carry them to the plug board associated with the patch panel. A satisfactory control can be obtained by using a patch panel, with its plug board, and a resistance dimmer board. This is modest stuff. More ambitious schemes will give extra ease and flexibility of control, but these advantages will be apparent to anyone who knows about stage lighting.

* *Unless of course a Pattern 264 Bifocal Spot is used.*

The plug board should reproduce the pattern of socket outlets in the lighting loft, and each circuit is then appropriately wired to the board, ending in a standard plug.

Since each area unit consists of three spotlights, these should be controlled by a single dimmer. On the patch panel a vertical row of sockets should be wired to each dimmer. In practice four rather than three sockets can be provided for each row; resistance dimmers are available to cope easily with a variable load of 1,000/2,000 watts, and special lights may often be used in relation to particular area units. Thus a total of twelve dimmers will usually be satisfactory for the sort of installation we have been describing. It allows up to 48 of the 60 available spotlights to be used at any one time. Further, the patching panel can be employed for rearrangements of the lights under control not only for each play but also, if required, during a play from cue to cue. Thus all 60 spotlights might be used during a single performance.

PRODUCTION-IN-THE-ROUND

It is useful to look further at the extreme form of open stage -- theatre-in-the-round. There is a clear progress in the series enclosed stage, open-end stage, thrust stage, theatre-in-the-round. And it is interesting to note that after so many enclosed stages our first open stage was the Mermaid, with an end stage; our second has been the Festival Theatre at Chichester, with its thrust stage; and, at present, there is no new building for theatre-in-the-round. However, I have worked in places converted for theatre-in-the-round, have seen many open stage productions of every sort, and feel that I can pick on some of the features of theatre-in-the-round that run through all open stages, more or less.

The most important feature of theatre-in-the-round is that it brings the emphasis of the presentation onto the actors, and that it restores to the actor the dignity of being a person in three dimensions. People who are worried about theatre-in-the-round because the audience must see the actors' backs are under the delusion that the actor only works with his front or that he is flat—rather like the loofah sponges that arrive nowadays, dried and flattened. The conventions of the enclosed stage may have flattened the actor in this way, but soak them in water, as it were, and they fill out into the most exciting of shapes. I believe that the actor is capable of three-dimensional expression in this way and that, further, his use of the space on the acting area should be dynamically related to the total space, and not restricted to the considerations of " picture ". It is only a flattened actor who needs to face his audience all the time, and if you put such an actor on an open stage he may rush into restless movement. But as he grows into a three-dimensional

*Production-in-the-round at Scarborough of " O'Flaherty, V.C.",
by Bernard Shaw.*

being he will realise that the only movement necessary on the open
stage is the movement that is necessary to his part, the play and
that is rooted in the essential business of communicating with the
audience.

But the actor expands in more ways than this. While considerations of " picture " can be best seen from the auditorium and the
producer alone will be able to direct the actors to best effect, the
dynamic movement of theatre-in-the-round will only ring true to
an audience if it is true to the actor; the producer can only say
whether it works or not. Thus the responsibility for creative work in
rehearsal is put on the actor. And, I believe, the actor can take full
responsibility for actual creative work in front of the audience at
the time of each performance. This is a complicated matter, difficult
to put in a mere sentence or two, but I believe that the audience is,
as it were, the canvas on which the actor paints and that this process
must be unique at each performance—no two audiences are the
same. If we could achieve the ideal level of creative acting in this
sense I think we should soon restore the drama to its rightful high
place among the arts—and audiences would go home and kick in
their television sets.

But if the actor is to have this vital impact upon the audience, he
must be well lit. This does not mean that more electricity is required
for theatre-in-the-round than for other forms of theatre. I lit my
first dozen productions of theatre-in-the-round out of a 15-amp.
plug, without overloading. After eight years my company still worked
with a board that had only four dimmers. It is a limitation. We
depend more on light than most theatres and, I think, we are
learning how to use it effectively. The actor must be lit so that all
the audience can see him; but, with an audience that is close, shadows

can be tremendously useful. The stabbing light of a few spotlights often has the intensity of drama that is missing from numerous and more powerful instruments whose brilliancy must compete with an illuminated background of scenery. When we have discovered more of the meaning of lighting in such terms as these, we shall be ready for a bigger distribution board, and my ideal theatre-in-the-round would include a preset control and 60, or so, ways— a luxury in a small theatre that would be modest with almost every other technical demand.

Some people are worried about the acoustics of the open stage. Acoustics is still, to some extent, a black art. But there is no reason why there should be any acoustical difficulties in a small theatre-in-the-round. When my company has performed in public halls we have often suffered from the architect's concern to reproduce a Roman swimming bath, a Greek temple, an Egyptian tomb, a renaissance palace or a Moorish alcazar. But no one need build a small theatre with bad acoustics, and I have seen many theatre-in-the-round productions in the United States where there is no difficulty whatever in hearing every word spoken by the actors, backs or no backs. It is necessary to build a theatre as a theatre if it is to be a successful theatre; which should surprise nobody.

A common criticism of theatre-in-the-round is that there is no scenery. This is true. But what is scenery for? It supplies a background to the actors, it suggests locale, it gives atmosphere. All these functions can be done by the actor with the help of lighting. On an enclosed stage there must be scenery to hide the spaces and machinery installed in order to handle scenery. But there are no such spaces and machinery to hide on the acting area of a theatre-in-the-round. Most plays are not about scenery but about actors, and the audience comes to see actors acting. However, scenery has always had a symbolic function. It represents the world background of the representative hero on the stage; it supplies a visual summary of the concept of the universe accepted at his particular time in history. The *décor simultané* supplies the medieval world picture. The cottage, forest and palace scenes of a few generations ago summarise an orderly and stratified society. The living room box sets of the last generation proclaim the wishful-thinking of a middle-class, middle-aged, middle-browed audience of frustrated people searching for comfort in an insecure world. In our day and age we have come to recognise that man not only has a back as well as a front, but that every action each person takes affects other people; we strive to communicate with each other, we feel lonely, but we are never alone and we cannot opt out of society no matter how terrible the newspaper headlines may be. The only possible background for a hero in this situation is a background of other people.

It is partly for reasons related to such a concept of performance that I like an arena as opposed to a stage. A stage elevates the actor and puts him on a pedestal; he looks down on his audience. This may be all right for a hero in classical tragedy, but it does not reflect the situation in most modern plays. The actor should be on the level with, as well as surrounded by, his audience.

In a very small theatre, where the actors are lit with economy, there is no need for make-up unless the actor is playing a part for which " disguise " is necessary. This may seem wrong, and certainly the convention of make-up is so strong that many actors do not feel properly equipped to go on stage without it. Disguise is the first technical device required by the actor. And it should be used, but used properly. Incidentally, costumes are very important in theatre-in-the-round and need careful work. The audience is close enough to see everything. So with make-up. If the actor has, as can be expected, a face, the audience will see it. It is an expressive instrument. If the part demands a mask or a disguise, the actor can put this on—and the audience will see what he sees when he looks in his mirror. But there is no need to use make-up as a convention to show people in the theatre merely that you do have a face. Once the actor accepts this, it gives him a wide range of subtle expression, takes the emphasis off his face and restores his confidence in his whole body, and makes of his relationship with the audience something intensely honest and open and immediate.

Finally, it is often said that theatre-in-the-round can only do a limited variety of plays. This is simply not true. Any play can be done in any form of theatre. It is no sillier to do Shaw's plays, which were written for an enclosed stage, in a theatre-in-the-round, than it is to do Shakespeare's, which were written for the open stage, on an enclosed stage. You may have tastes, and prefer one sort of play in a particular sort of theatre but you can hardly develop taste without something to get your teeth into; one man's meat is another man's poison; and the theatre, anyhow, should provide a rich diet of good things. I have no patience with theoretical limitations imposed by ignorant authorities. Besides, I believe that the most important plays are new plays, and why pour new wine into old bottles?

After that plea for an open mind toward the open stage, I hesitate to make a final summary that will bring back the other forms of theatre included in this book. It seems to me that each of the forms of open stage has certain distinct advantages. These can best be pointed at if I suggest that the enclosed stage is probably best for spectacular plays, the open-end stage for satirical plays where the actors stand half-way between the real audience and the artificial world built by the playwright, the thrust stage for classical and heroic plays depending primarily on language, and theatre-in-the-round for modern plays where the relationships between characters have the appearance of reality and where the thematic material is of immediate concern to the audience. Let us get all forms flourishing and investigate further this serious business of entertainment, excitement and delight.

A2 INDEX OF PHOTOGRAPHS & DIAGRAMS

Photographs

Photograph 1	Stephen Joseph	page	16
Photograph 2	The Library Theatre 1950s	page	17
Photograph 3	The Library Theatre 1970s	page	19
Photograph 4	Alan Ayckbourn 1957	page	20
Photograph 5	Alan Ayckbourn and Ken Boden renaming the Scarborough Theatre in 1978	page	21
Photograph 6	Sir Alan Ayckbourn 1990s	page	22
Photograph 7	Vom Lighting: *Love Off The Shelf*	page	36
Photograph 8	Numerous hanging practicals	page	38
Photograph 9	Set pieces obscuring the rig	page	39
Photograph 10	Using colour: *Gaslight*	page	42
Photograph 11	Numerous keylights: *Conversations With My Father*	page	49
Photograph 12	Relying on Practicals: *Rocket To The Moon*	page	51
Photograph 13	*Mr. A's Amazing Maze Plays*	page	53
Photograph 14	Ground plans of light: *Village Fete*	page	56
Photograph 15	Lighting for fun: *Love Off The Shelf*	page	60
Photograph 16	*Travels With My Aunt*	page	67
Photograph 17	*Travels With My Aunt*	page	68
Photograph 18	Crowded grid	page	72
Photograph 19	New Victoria Theatre grid	page	73
Photograph 20	Stephen Joseph Theatre (Westborough) grid	page	74
Photograph 21	The Beam	page	77
Photograph 22	*Haunting Julia* set	page	79
Photograph 23	*Love Off The Shelf* cliff top scene	page	82
Photograph 24	Kath Geraghty	page	111
Photograph 25	David Taylor	page	117
Photograph 26	*Animal Island* at The Drum Theatre	page	118

Photograph 27   *All In The Wrong* at The Orange Tree   page 121
Photograph 28   Jo Dawson   page 125
Photograph 29   *Oliver Twist* at The New Victoria Theatre   page 131
Photograph 30   Stephen Joseph   page 138

Diagrams

Figure 1	Control room design	page	18
Figure 2	The 45° / 90° rule	page	26
Figure 3	9 stage areas	page	26
Figure 4	Cutting off the far side focus	page	27
Figure 5	9 area general cover	page	28
Figure 6	The 120° rule	page	30
Figure 7	13 area hexagonal stage	page	30
Figure 8	13 area general cover	page	31
Figure 9	Backlight position demonstration	page	35
Figure 10	Using a section to predict shadows	page	37
Figure 11	*Love Off The Shelf* rig plan	page	58
Figure 12	Symmetrical rig plan: *Dreams From A Summerhouse*	page	63
Figure 13	Calculating downlighter quantity	page	76
Figure 14	Cantata under the beam: *Village Fete*	page	78
Figure 15	*Haunting Julia* rig plan	page	80
Figure 16	*Calisto 5* set sketch	page	92
Figure 17	Section Drawing A: 45 degree rule	page	96
Figure 18	Section Drawing B: cheating the rule	page	98
Figure 19	Section Drawing C: staircase angles	page	100
Figure 20	Sketch of *Feed* set	page	101
Figure 21	*The Musical Jigsaw Play* rig plan	page	103
Figure 22	Two *Weeks With The Queen* rig plan	page	104
Figure 23	Sketch demonstrating two colour general rig	page	113
Figure 24	*Animal Island* rig plan	page	119
Figure 25	*All In The Wrong* rig plan (The Orange Tree)	page	123
Figure 26	Section through The Royal Exchange Theatre	page	124
Figure 27	The New Victoria Theatre grid and patch plan	page	127

A3 RESUME OF DESIGN EXAMPLES

The comments and observations that I have made in this book have been drawn from my conclusions after seven years at the Stephen Joseph Theatre, and from conversations with other lighting designers working in this particular staging format. The following is a bibliography of those experiences:

Jackie Staines
Stephen Joseph Theatre In The Round

June Moon
(Period Drama) Director: Alan Strachan, Musical Director: John Pattison

Invisible Friends
(Children's Drama) Director: Alan Ayckbourn

Alphabetical Order
(Comedy) Director: Alan Strachan

This Is Where We Came In
(Children's Show) Director: Alan Ayckbourn,
Musical Director: John Pattison

The Price
(Period Drama) Director: Caroline Smith

Calisto 5
(Family Show) Director: Alan Ayckbourn, Musical Director: John Pattison

Same Time Next Year
(Comedy/Drama) Director: Malcolm Hebden

The Village Fete
(Comedy/Drama) Director: Alan Ayckbourn,
Musical Director: John Pattison

Rutherford And Son
(Period Drama) Director: Malcolm Hebden

My Very Own Story
(Children's Show) Director: Alan Ayckbourn,
Musical Director: John Pattison

To
(Modern Drama) Director: Malclom Hebden

Dangerous Obsession
(Thriller) Director: Malcolm Hebden

This Is Where We Came In
(Children's show) Director: Alan Ayckbourn,
Musical Director: John Pattison

Confusions
(5 one act plays) Director: Malcolm Hebden

Neville's Island
(Comedy/Drama) Director: Connal Orton

Rocket To The Moon
(Period Drama) Director: Malcolm Hebden

Dreams From A Summerhouse
(Musical) Director: Alan Ayckbourn,
Musical Director: John Pattison

Abigail's Party
(Comedy) Director: Malcolm Hebden

My Very Own Story
(Children's Show) Director: Alan Ayckbourn,
Musical Director: John Pattison

Prince On A White Bike
(Period Drama) Director: Connal Orton

Feed
(Period Comedy/Drama/Musical) Director: James Tomlinson,
Musical Director: John Pattison

Table Manners
(Comedy) Director: Alan Ayckbourn

Living Together
(Comedy) Director: Alan Ayckbourn

Round And Round The Garden
(Comedy) Director: Alan Ayckbourn

Physical Jerks
(Comedy) Director: Connal Orton

Love Off The Shelf
(Comedy Musical) Director: Alan Ayckbourn,
Musical Director: John Pattison

Mr. A's Amazing Maze Plays
(Family Show) Director: Malcolm Hebden

The End Of The Food Chain
(Comedy/Drama) Director: Connal Orton

Haunting Julia
(Thriller) Director: Alan Ayckbourn

Gaslight
(Period Thriller) Director: Malcolm Hebden

Penny Blue
(Comedy/Drama) Director: Malcolm Hebden

Two Weeks With The Queen
(Comedy/Drama) Director: Alan Ayckbourn,
Musical Director: John Pattison

Conversations With My Father
(Comedy/Drama) Director: Alan Ayckbourn

The Musical Jigsaw Play
(Family Show/Musical) Director: Alan Ayckbourn,
Musical Director: John Pattison

Oleanna
(Drama) Director: Malcolm Hebden

The Old Laundry Theatre
Table Manners
(Comedy) Director: Alan Ayckbourn

Living Together
(Comedy) Director: Alan Ayckbourn

Round And Round The Garden
(Comedy) Director: Alan Ayckbourn

Haunting Julia
(Thriller) Director: Alan Ayckbourn

Two Weeks With The Queen
(Comedy/Drama) Director: Alan Ayckbourn,
Musical Director: John Pattison

The Musical Jigsaw Play
(Family Show/Musical) Director: Alan Ayckbourn
Musical Director: John Pattison

The Royal National Theatre (Cottesloe)
Two Weeks With The Queen
(Comedy/Drama) Director: Alan Ayckbourn,
Musical Director: John Pattison

Mick Hughes
Stephen Joseph Theatre-In-The-Round (Westwood)
Revenger's Comedies
(Comedy/Drama) Director: Alan Ayckbourn

Body Language
(Comedy/Drama) Director: Alan Ayckbourn

Othello
(Period Tragedy) Director: Alan Ayckbourn

Wildest Dreams
(Comedy/Drama) Director: Alan Ayckbourn

Taking Steps
(Comedy) Director: Alan Ayckbourn

Time of My Life
(Comedy/Drama) Director: Alan Ayckbourn

Communicating Doors
(Comedy/Drama) Director: Alan Ayckbourn

A Word From Our Sponsor
(Musical) Director: Alan Ayckbourn
          Musical Director: John Pattison

The Round (SJT Westborough)
By Jeeves
(Musical) Director: Alan Ayckbourn,
        Musical Director: Andrew Lloyd Webber

Kath Geraghty
Stephen Joseph Theatre-In-The-Round (Westwood)
Let's Pretend
(Modern Drama) Director: Malcolm Hebden

Hard Times
(Period Drama) Director: Kate Valentine

The Round (SJT Westborough)
Love Me Slender
(Modern Drama) Director: Auriol Smith

They're Playing Our Song
(Musical) Director: Alan Ayckbourn,
Musical Director: Simon Cryer

Honk!
(Family Show) Director: Julia McKenzie,
Musical Director: John Pattison

Knights In Plastic Armour
(Drama) Director: Alan Ayckbourn

Calisto 7
(Family Show) Director: Alan Ayckbourn,
Musical Director: Simon Cryer

Private Lives
(Period Comedy/Drama) Director: Sam Walters

Perfect Pitch
(Comedy) Director: John Godber

Comic Potential
(Comedy) Director: Alan Ayckbourn

What Every Woman Knows
(Period Drama) Director: Robin Herford

New Vic Theatre
Perfect Pitch
(Comedy) Director : John Godber
Comic Potential
(Comedy) Director: Alan Ayckbourn

The Old Laundry Theatre
Comic Potential
(Comedy) Director: Alan Ayckbourn

David Taylor
The Orange Tree
All In The Wrong
(Restoration comedy) Director: Sam Walters

The Drum Theatre Royal Plymouth
Animal Island
(Family Musical) Director: Amanda Knott
Brother Jacques
(Large Musical) Director: Nick Stimpson

The Man In The Moon
Hamlet
(Drama) Director: Alistair Middleton

The Royal Albert Hall
A Celebration of Christmas
(Music and Drama Special) Director: Jane Glover

Jo Dawson
New Victoria
Waiting For Godot
(Play)   Director: Ensemble
A Bedroom Farce
(Comedy) Director: Rob Swain

Dear Nobody
(Play) Director: Rob Swain

Private Lives
(Play) Director: Chris Martin

Beauty & The Beast
(Christmas Show) Director: Peter Cheeseman

Overture
(Play) Director: Peter Cheeseman

HMS Pinafore
(Musical) Director: Peter Cheeseman

Oliver Twist
(Play) Director: Chris Martin

Return To The Forbidden Planet
(Rock & Roll Musical) Director: Rob Swain

Arms And The Man
(Play) Director: Peter Cheeseman

Aladdin
(Christmas Show) Director: Chris Martin

Insignificance
(Play) Director: Rob Swain

The Tempest
(Play) Director: Peter Cheeseman

Translations
(Play) Director: Roxanna Silbert

Kiss Of The Spiderwoman
(Play) Director: Michael Cashman

New Vic Theatre
Othello
(Play) Director: Gwenda Hughes

Dead Funny
(Play) Director: Kevin Knight

She Knows You Know
(Musical Play) Director: Gwenda Hughes

Travels With My Aunt
(Play) Director: Natalie Wilson

Office Suite
(Two Plays) Director: Gwenda Hughes

Neville's Island
(Play) Director: Gwenda Hughes

A Midsummer Night's Dream
(Play) Director: Natalie Wilson

Wizard Of Oz
(Musical) Director: Gwenda Hughes

Loot
(Play) Director: Natalie Wilson

Moll Flanders
(Musical) Director: Gwenda Hughes

Who's Afraid Of Virginia Woolfe
(Play) Director: Gwenda Hughes

From A Jack To A King
(Rock & Roll Musical) Director: Rob Swain

Second To Last In The Sack Race
(Play) Director: Laurie Sasom

The Mikado
(Musical) Director: Chris Monk

The Round (SJT)
The Mikado
(Musical) Director: Chris Monk

 **'ROUND' VENUES IN GREAT BRITAIN**

Dedicated 'in-the-round' Venues

The Library Theatre, Scarborough (1955-1976)
Vernon Street, Scarborough, North Yorkshire

Theatre-in-the-Round at Westwood
Stephen Joseph Theatre-in-the-Round (1976-1996)
Valley Bridge Parade, Scarborough, North Yorkshire YO11 2PL

The Round (1996 – date)
Stephen Joseph Theatre
Westborough, Scarborough, North Yorkshire YO11 1JW
01723 370540
http://www.sjt.uk.com

The Victoria Theatre, Stoke-on-Trent (1962-1981)
New Victoria (1981-1998)
New Vic Theatre (1998 – date)
Etruria Road, Newcastle-under-Lyme, Staffs ST5 0JG
01782 717954
http://www.uktw.co.uk/info/newvic.htm

Royal Exchange Theatre, Manchester
St. Ann's Square, Manchester, M2 7DH
0161 833 9938
http://www.royalexchange.co.uk/

The Old Laundry Theatre,
Bowness-on-Windermere, Cumbria LA23 3BX
015394 88444

The Orange Tree
1 Clarence Street, Richmond,
Surrey TW9 2SA
020 8940 3633

Variable staging format venues
Brentwood Theatre
15b Shenfield Road, Brentwood, Essex CM15 8AG
01277-230833
www.brentwoodtheatre.freeserve.co.uk

Arnolfini
6 Narrow Quay, Bristol, Avon BS1 4QA
0117 9299191
http://www.arnolfini.demon.co.uk

GilmorehillG12
9 University Avenue, Glasgow G12 8QQ
0141-330 5522
http://www.gla.ac.uk/ghcentre

Bristol New Vic
Bristol Old Vic, King Street, Bristol BS1 4ED
0117 9493993
http://www.bristol.old.vic.uk

Nuffield Theatre
Lancaster University,
Bailrigg, Lancaster, Lancs LA1 4YW
01524 594151
http://www.lancs.ac.uk/users/Nuffield

De Montfort Hall
Granville Road, Leicester LE1 7RU
(0116) 233 3113

Watermill Theatre
Bagnor, Newbury, Berks RG20 8AE
01635 45834
http://www.watermill.org.uk

Bonington Theatre
High Street, Arnold, Nottingham NG5 7EE
0115 9670114

The Pit
Barbican Centre, Silk Street, London EC2Y 8BQ
020 7628 8264
http://www.barbican.org.uk/

Questors Theatre
Mattock Lane, Ealing, London W5 5BQ
020 8567 0011
http://www.questors.org.uk

The Octagon
Howell Croft South, Bolton BL1 1SB
01204 29407

The Drum (Theatre Royal)
Royal Parade, Plymouth PL1 2TR
01752 668282

The Cottesloe (Royal National Theatre)
South Bank, London SE1 9PX
020 7928 2033

College Venues
East Yorkshire Coast College Theatre-in-the-Round
(Formally the Stephen Joseph Theatre)
Valley Bridge Parade, Scarborough, North Yorkshire YO11 2PL

Grange Arts Centre
Rochdale Road, Oldham OL9 6AA
0161 785 4239

The Rose Theatre, Rose Bruford College
Lamorbey Park, Sidcup, Kent DA15 9DF
020 8300 3024
http://www.bruford.ac.uk

A5 BIBLIOGRAPHY AND FURTHER READING

Books

Theatre in the Round
Stephen Joseph
Barrie & Rockcliff, 1967

New Theatre Forms
Stephen Joseph
Sir Isaac Pitman & Sons, 1968

The Story Of The Playhouse In England
Stephen Joseph
Barrie & Rockcliff, 1963

Actor and Architect
Tyrone Guthrie, Richard Southern, Sean Kenny, Christopher Stevens, Hugh Hunt and John English, edited by Stephen Joseph
Manchester University Press, 1964

Planning For New Theatre Forms
Stephen Joseph
The Strand Electric and Engineering Co. Ltd.
First edition: 1962 and later editions

Adaptable Theatres
edited by Stephen Joseph
Association of British Theatre Technicians, 1962

A Method of Lighting The Stage
Stanley McCandless
Theatre Arts Books New York, 4th edition 1958

Stephen Joseph Theatre
A Photographic Record of the Conversion of the Odeon Cinema, Scarborough
Photography by Adrian Gatie and Commentary by Alan Ayckbourn
Stephen Joseph Theatre, 1996

The Art Of Stage Lighting
Fred Bentham
Pitman Publishing, 1968 and later editions.

Stage Lighing
Richard Pilbrow
Studio Vista, 1970 and later editions

Stage Lighing Design
Richard Pilbrow
By Design Press, New York 1997
Nick Hern Books, 1997

The Stage Lighting Handbook
Francis Reid
Adam and Charles Black, 1976 and later editions

Lighting The Stage
Francis Reid
Focal Press, 1995

Lighting by Design
Brian Fitt and Joe Thornley
Focal Press, 1992

Conversations With Ayckbourn
Ian Watson
MacDonald, 1981

Articles

Lighting In The Round
Jackie Staines
Lighting + Sound International, August 1991

Ayckbourn and The Odeon 'Building Around Talent'
John Offord
Lighting + Sound International, June 1993

Communicating Doors
Jackie Staines
Lighting + Sound International, February 1994

Royal's Curtain Rises Again
Andy Hayles
Lighting + Sound International, January 1999

A Diversion From Reality
Jackie Staines
Focus - the ALD magazine, Issue 14

Scarborough By Gaslight
Michael Northen
Focus, October 1994

INDEX

120° rule 18, 27-32, 113-114, 122-126, 151

13 area general cover 151

13 area hexagonal stage 151

45 degree rule 96, 151

45° / 90° rule 151

45° rule 25, 28, 97, 98, 151

60° offset 29

9 area general cover 151

9 stage areas 151

90 rule 25, 32, 122

90° rule 26, 28, 30, 113, 151

A Bedroom Farce 158

A Celebration of Christmas 158

A Diversion From Reality 167

A Method of Lighting The Stage 165

A Midsummer Night's Dream 159

A Phoenix Too Frequent 13

A Photographic Record of the Conversion of the Odeon 166

A Word From Our Sponsor 156

Abiding Passions 89

Abigail's Party 154

Actor and Architect 165

Adaptable Theatres 165

Air-conditioning 53, 132

Aladdin 159

Albert Bridge 108

ALD 42, 167

All In The Wrong 120-123, 150-151, 158

Alphabetical Order 153

Animal Island 118, 119, 122, 150, 158

Animal Island rig plan 151

Arena stage 13, 15, 25, 122

Arms And The Man 159

Arnolfini 162

Art Deco 73

Association of British Theatre Technicians (ABTT) 17, 165

Association of Lighting Designers 42

Auriol Smith 157

Ayckbourn, Alan 11, 20-23, 48, 52, 57, 107-111, 149, 153-158, 166, 167

Ayckbourn and The Odeon 'Building Around Talent' 167

Backlight 31-37, 51, 100, 114, 120, 128, 130, 151

Backlight position demonstration 151

Bamboozler 91, 92

Battery powered 85, 89

Beam (Structural) 59, 76-78, 91, 149, 151

Beam splitter gobo 91

Beauty & The Beast 158

Bentham, Fred 166

Birdies 50, 51, 59-64, 81-91, 102

Black gloss floor 83

Bleacher 104

Boden, Ken 14, 21, 22, 23, 149

Body Language 108, 149, 156

Bonington Theatre 163

Brentwood Theatre 162

Bristol New Vic 162

Broadway Pink 57

Brother Jacques 158

Brown, Jan Bee 36, 41, 60, 79, 82

BT exchange 94

Bubble wrap 94

By Jeeves 111, 156

Cabling 71, 75, 84-86, 93, 95, 128

Calculating downlighter quantity 151

Calisto 5 92-95, 110, 151, 153

Calisto 7 157

Cambridge University 13

Cantata under the beam 151

Canvas 55, 57, 67, 68, 97, 130

Cashman, Michael 159

Catwalks 73-74, 104, 117-119, 123-127

CCTV 95

Central School of Speech and Drama 13, 14

Cheeseman, Peter 128, 132, 158, 159
Claysmore 13
Coda floods 64, 87
Colour wheels 37, 62
Comic Potential 157, 158
Communicating Doors 110, 111, 156, 167
Composite gobos 59, 72, 77
Condie, Sue 67, 68, 131
Confusions 154
Control room design 18, 151
Conversations With Ayckbourn 166
Conversations With My Father 48, 49,
    87-91, 99, 110, 111, 120, 149, 155
Cottesloe Theatre 26, 97, 103-105, 121,
    156, 163
Cross-wash 29, 32-33, 37, 41, 61-64,
    102, 129
Crowded grid 149
Crucible Theatre 94
Cryer, Simon 157

Cutting off the far side focus 151
Dangerous Obsession 154
Dawson, Jo
    60, 67, 68, 121, 131, 150, 158
De Montfort Hall 162
Dead Funny 159
Dear Nobody 158
Dee, Janie 86, 149
Designing General Cover 25
DHA 91
Director of Productions 22
Dreams From A Summerhouse 39, 61-64,
    85, 86, 117, 131, 149, 151, 154
Drum Theatre 117-119, 150, 158, 163
Dry ice 52, 53, 59, 61, 82, 85

East Yorkshire Coast College 18
East Yorkshire Coast College Theatre-in-the-
    Round 163
Effects, Pyrotechnics and Smoke 52
Egg crates 104
Electric doilies 89, 90
Elevations 26, 37, 38, 50, 76, 96
Embassy Studio 117

English Heritage 73, 114
English, John 165
Entertaining Mr. Sloane 120
Ethernet 125
Excess spill 102
Eye fatigue 48, 63

Far side focus 27
Feed 96, 101, 154
Finding Enough Positions 72
Firework display 64
Fishpond pump 88
Fitt, Brian 166
Flare 57, 83
Flicker effect 87
Flicker-candles 88
Floor 54, 72, 81-93, 97, 99, 101
Fluorescent 42, 52
Flying pieces 27, 32, 39, 49, 50,
    71-77, 82-83, 87, 91, 96, 99,
    133
Flying Pieces and Tall Actors 96
Focus 42
Fog 64, 65
Follow-on cues 48
Followspot
    59, 116, 119, 122, 129, 132
Fountain 65, 88, 109
Freak weather conditions 94
From A Jack To A King 160
Frontlight 35, 37, 120, 130

Gambon, Michael 109
Gaslight 40-43, 48, 67, 68, 83,
    86, 111, 149, 155
Gatie, Adrian 38, 39, 41, 49, 53, 74,
    79, 86, 107, 109, 166
Gauze 61, 81, 82
General cover 25-42, 47, 56-58,
    63-65, 71, 79-80, 96-100, 105,
    107, 109, 112-116, 123-126,
    132, 133, 151
Geraghty, Kath 33, 52, 67, 111-116,
    125, 126, 130, 132, 149, 157

Gilmorehill G12 162
Gingold, Hermione 13, 14
Gloss 42, 55, 57, 83
Glossop 107, 108, 109, 111
Glover, Jane 158
Gobo projection 55, 56, 57, 75
Gobo wash 40, 76, 96, 128, 129
Gobo Washes Galore 75
Godber, John 157
Grange Arts Centre 164
Grid Obstacles 76
Ground plans of light 149
Guthrie, Tyrone 165

Hamburg frost 37
Hamlet 158
Hard patch 18, 71, 125
Hard Times 157
Harrogate Theatre 66
Haunting Julia 79, 80, 87-92, 111,
      149, 151, 155
Hayles, Andy 167
Haze 64
Hebden, Malcolm
      42, 44, 153, 154, 155, 157
Herford, Robin 157
Hexagonal stage 30, 151
Hickling, Alfred 66
HMS Pinafore 159
Holt, Michael 60, 88, 109
Honk! 157
How Special Are Specials? 47
Hughes, Gwenda 128, 159, 160
Hughes, Mick 65, 88, 107 - 114,
      125, 149, 156
Hunt, Hugh 165

Insignificance 159
Invisible Friends 153

Joseph, Michael 13
Joseph, Stephen 11- 23, 27, 29, 32,
      40, 48, 73, 98, 107, 113, 117, 1
      35, 137, 138, 149, 150, 165

JR Clancy 74
Juke box 87
June Moon 153
Just Between Ourselves 19, 20

Kenny, Sean 165
Keylight 33, 34, 41, 47, 48, 52,
      62-65, 81-85, 130, 131, 149
King, Peter 116
Kiss Of The Spiderwoman 159
KK wheels 92
Knight, Kevin 159
Knights In Plastic Armour 157
Knott, Amanda 158

Lake Windermere 65
Let's Pretend 157
Lewry, Fiona 109
Library Theatre 15-20, 113, 149, 161
Lightboxes 96, 101
Lighting by Design 166
Lighting for Darkness 61
Lighting for Fun 57, 149
Lighting In The Round 167
Lighting The Stage 166
Littlevoice 128
Living Together 154, 155
Lloyd Webber, Andrew 156
Loot 160
Love Me Slender 157
Love Off The Shelf 36, 37, 57-60,
      82, 85, 149, 151, 155
Macbeth 61, 65
Mackintosh, Iain 122
Mahatma Ghandi building 14
Man In The Moon Theatre 158
Man Of The Moment 65, 90
Markland, Sara 37
Martin, Chris 158, 159
McCandless, Stanley 25, 28, 165
McKenzie, Julia 157
Memorial service 135
Middleton, Alistair 158
Mills & Boon 57
Moll Flanders 160

Monk, Chris 160
Monsters 94
Moonlight 47, 62-64, 117, 131, 132
Mr. A's Amazing Maze Plays
    52, 53, 67, 85, 149, 155
Municipal Library 73
Musical Jigsaw Play, The 90, 102, 103,
    111, 151, 155, 156
My Very Own Story 154

National Theatre 22, 26, 103, 111, 156
Neville's Island
    53, 61, 64, 65, 87, 154, 159
New Theatre Forms 165
New Vic Theatre 125, 128, 157-161
New Victoria 73, 127, 131, 149-151,
    158, 161
Nichols, Juliet 38, 39, 51, 56, 86
Nightmares From Round Street 71
Northen, Michael 42, 167
Nuffield Theatre 162
Numerous hanging practicals 149
Numerous keylights 149

Octagon Theatre 163
Odeon 22, 23, 45, 72, 73, 74, 112, 114
Odeon conversion 73
Office Suite 159
Offord, John 167
Oil lamps 89, 90
Old Laundry Theatre
    26, 97, 102, 111, 155, 158, 161
Oleanna 111, 155
Oliver Twist 130, 131, 150, 159
One Over the Eight 110
Open white 40, 56, 102
Orange Tree Theatre
    117, 120, 121, 122, 123, 150,
    151 158, 162
Orton, Connal 154, 155
Othello 61, 65, 88, 111, 156, 159
Othello: The Play 109
Overture 159

Painting The Stage 55
Passing ferry 64
Patch table 108
Patching Large Rigs 71
Pattison, John 91, 153-157
Pendant light fittings 27, 38, 39, 85
Penny Blue 111, 155
Perfect Pitch 117, 131, 132, 157
Photo-electric cell 89
Physical Jerks 154
Pilbrow, Richard 166
Pin spot 72, 99
Planning For New Theatre Forms 165
Practical cover 89, 120
Practicals 47, 51, 62-66, 71, 84-92,
    96, 110, 149
Practicals and Problems 84
Preset lighting 44, 83
Price, Kenneth 51
Prince On A White Bike 154
Private Lives 157, 158
Projection 57, 83, 115, 116
Pyroflash 95
Pyrotechnics 53, 92, 93, 95

Questors Theatre 163

Reich & Vogel 119, 122
Reid, Francis 166
Relying on Practicals 149
Return To The Forbidden Planet 159
Revenger's Comedies 107, 156
Revolves 32, 57, 58, 59, 82, 85
Rocket To The Moon
    38, 39, 51, 85, 99, 149, 154
Ropelight 87, 96
Rose Bruford College
    30, 34, 105, 126, 164
Rose Theatre 30, 34, 97, 126, 164
Round And Round The Garden
    154, 155
Royal Albert Hall 158
Royal Exchange 124, 125, 151, 161
Royal National Theatre
    26, 103, 156, 163

Royal's Curtain Rises Again 167
Russell, Alan 74
Rutherford And Son 153

Same Time Next Year 110, 153
Sasom, Laurie 160
Scarborough By Gaslight 167
Scarborough Evening News 15, 16
Scarborough public library 14
Scarborough Technical College 95
Scarborough Theatre Trust 14, 22
Sceno Plus 74
Scrollers 58-59, 102, 112, 115, 122,
    125, 126, 129
Sea-fret 65
Second To Last In The Sack Race 128, 160
Sections 26, 29, 37, 38, 76, 96, 98-100,
    124, 151
Set pieces obscuring the rig 149
Shadow 27, 37-39, 61-66, 75, 80, 92,
    97, 98, 115
She Knows You Know 159
Shiny floor 83
Silbert, Roxanna 159
Simon Cryer 157
Size Isn't Everything 79
SJT 39, 41, 71, 72, 113, 156, 157, 160
Sketch demonstrating two colour general
    rig 151
Sketch of *Feed* set 151
Smith, Caroline 153
Smoke 52, 53, 64, 66, 87, 91, 120
Smoke plume 54
Society of Theatre Consultants 17
Southern, Richard 165
Special effects 23, 47, 52, 53, 96
Specials 19, 22, 25, 28-29, 32, 37, 47,
    51
Square-shaped stage 28
Stage Lighing 166
Stage Lighing Design 166
Staines, Jackie 42, 66, 153, 167
Staircase 81, 100, 102, 151
Staircases 99
Stairway 100

Stairwell 102
Stephen Joseph Theatre
    11, 22, 26, 32, 33, 37, 39,
    42, 52, 72-77, 84, 97, 100,
    103, 107, 110, 111, 114,
    127, 149, 153, 156, 157, 161
Stephen Joseph Theatre Company 22
Stephen Joseph Theatre A Photographic
    Record of the Odeon Conversion
    166
Stevens, Christopher 165
Stimpson, Nick 158
Strachan, Alan 153
Sunrise 62
Sunset 62
Swain, Rob 158, 159, 160
Swimming pool 65

Table Manners 154, 155
TABS 135, 137
Taking Steps 92, 93, 94, 110, 156
Tall actors 71, 96
Taylor, David 117-119, 150, 158
Tensioned wire grid 22, 83, 114
The Art Of Stage Lighting 166
The Ballroom 116
The Beauty of Symmetry 102
The End Of The Food Chain
    61, 63, 87, 155
The Mikado 128, 129, 132, 160
The Pit 163
The Price 153
The Round 156, 157, 160, 161
The Stage Lighting Handbook 166
The Story Of The Playhouse In England
    165
The Tempest 159
The Times 13
Theatre in the Round 165
Theatre In The Round At Westwood 20
Theatre Projects Consulants 74, 117,
    122, 124
They're Playing Our Song 157
This Is Where We Came In
    76, 153, 154

Thornley, Joe 166
Time And Time Again 65
Time of My Life 110, 156
To 154
Tomlinson, James 154
Trampoline 22, 74, 114
Transformation 79, 81
Translations 159
Travels With My Aunt 60, 67, 68, 149, 159
Tripe 87
Truck 51, 64, 65, 87, 88
Two colour general cover 33, 113, 114
Two colour wash 29, 32, 114
Two Cover, or Not Two Cover 32
Two covers 40
Two Weeks With The Queen 102-105, 111, 151, 155, 156

Ultra-violet 52
Underwater cue lights 90
Up-lighters 81
Using a section to predict shadows 151
Using colour 149
Using Colour in the General Cover 40
Using Sections and Elevations 37
Using the Floor as a Canvas 67
UV 52

Valentine, Kate 157
Vari*Lite 59, 111
Variegated 25, 41
Varnish 57, 83
Victoria Theatre 161
Video 92, 93, 94, 95
Video game 94
Village Fete, The 55-57, 67, 77-78, 83, 149, 153
Vom lighting 149
vom roof 102
Vom wall 37, 102
Voms 88, 99, 100, 102, 105, 128, 130

Waiting For Godot 158
Walls, Stairs and Voms 99

Walters, Sam 120, 157, 158
Watermill Theatre 163
Watson, Ian 166
Way Upstream 65
Westborough 22, 23, 72, 74, 113-116, 149, 156, 157
Westwood 18, 20-27, 39, 53, 59, 71-77, 100, 107, 112-114, 122, 157, 161
What Every Woman Knows 157
What is Backlight Anyway 33
What is Keylight in-the-round? 47
Who's Afraid Of The Virginia Woolfe 160
Wildest Dreams 110, 156
Wilson, Nataile 159, 160
Wire mesh grid 74, 75, 124, 132
Wizard Of Oz 128, 160
Wood, John 13
Wrea Head 13
Wurlitzer 50

ENTERTAINMENT TECHNOLOGY PRESS

FREE SUBSCRIPTION SERVICE

Keeping Up To Date with

Lighting Techniques For Theatre-In-The-Round

Entertainment Technology Press titles are continually up-dated, and all changes and additions are listed in date order in the relevant dedicated area of the publisher's website. Simply go to the front page of www.etnow.com and click on the BOOKS button. From there you can locate the title and be connected through to the latest information and services related to the publication.

The author hopes to add further in-the-round production examples from other lighting designers to future editions of this book, and contributions for possible inclusion are welcomed. Also, comments on this title, any further information on in-the-round venues and details of research on the subject will also be appreciated. Please contact the author by email on book@lightingsolution.co.uk

Titles Published by Entertainment Technology Press

ABC of Theatre Jargon *Francis Reid* **£9.95** ISBN 1904031099
This glossary of theatrical terminology explains the common words and phrases that are used in normal conversation between actors, directors, designers, technicians and managers.

Aluminium Structures in the Entertainment Industry *Peter Hind* **£24.95**
ISBN 1904031064
Aluminium Structures in the Entertainment Industry aims to educate the reader in all aspects of the design and safe usage of temporary and permanent aluminium structures specific to the entertainment industry – such as roof structures, PA towers, temporary staging, etc.

AutoCAD 2010 – A Handbook for Theatre Users *David Ripley* **£24.95** ISBN 9781904031611
From 'Setting Up' to 'Drawing in Three Dimensions' via 'Drawings Within Drawings', this compact and fully illustrated guide to AutoCAD covers everything from the basics to full colour rendering and remote plotting. Title completely revised in June 2010.

Automation in the Entertainment Industry – A User's Guide *Mark Ager and John Hastie* **£29.95** ISBN 9781904031581
In the last 15 years, there has been a massive growth in the use of automation in entertainment, especially in theatres, and it is now recognised as its own discipline. However, it is still only used in around 5% of theatres worldwide. In the next 25 years, given current growth patterns, that figure will rise to 30%. This will mean that the majority of theatre personnel, including directors, designers, technical staff, actors and theatre management, will come into contact with automation for the first time at some point in their careers. This book is intended to provide insights and practical advice from those who use automation, to help the first-time user understand the issues and avoid the pitfalls in its implementation. In the past, theatre automation was seen by many as a complex, unreliable and expensive toy, not for general use. The aim of this book is to dispel that myth.

Basics – A Beginner's Guide to Lighting Design *Peter Coleman* **£9.95** ISBN 1904031412
The fourth in the author's 'Basics' series, this title covers the subject area in four main sections: The Concept, Practical Matters, Related Issues and The Design Into Practice. In an area that is difficult to be definitive, there are several things that cross all the boundaries of all lighting design and it's these areas that the author seeks to help with.

Basics – A Beginner's Guide to Special Effects *Peter Coleman* **£9.95** ISBN 1904031331
This title introduces newcomers to the world of special effects. It describes all types of special effects including pyrotechnic, smoke and lighting effects, projections, noise machines, etc. It places emphasis on the safe storage, handling and use of pyrotechnics.

Basics – A Beginner's Guide to Stage Lighting *Peter Coleman* **£9.95** ISBN 190403120X
This title does what it says: it introduces newcomers to the world of stage lighting. It will not teach the reader the art of lighting design, but will teach beginners much about the 'nuts and bolts' of stage lighting.

Basics: A Beginner's Guide to Stage Management *Peter Coleman* **£7.95**
ISBN 9781904031475
The fifth in Peter Coleman's popular 'Basics' series, this title provides a practical insight
into, and the definition of, the role of stage management. Further chapters describe Cueing
or 'Calling' the Show (the Prompt Book), and the Hardware and Training for Stage
Management. This is a book about people and systems, without which most of the technical
equipment used by others in the performance workplace couldn't function.

Basics – A Beginner's Guide to Stage Sound *Peter Coleman* **£9.95** ISBN 1904031277
This title does what it says: it introduces newcomers to the world of stage sound. It will not
teach the reader the art of sound design, but will teach beginners much about the background
to sound reproduction in a theatrical environment.

Building Better Theaters *Michael Mell* **£16.95** 1904031404
A title within our Consultancy Series, this book describes the process of designing a theater,
from the initial decision to build through to opening night. Michael Mell's book provides
a step-by-step guide to the design and construction of performing arts facilities. Chapters
discuss: assembling your team, selecting an architect, different construction methods, the
architectural design process, construction of the theater, theatrical systems and equipment,
the stage, backstage, the auditorium, ADA requirements and the lobby. Each chapter
clearly describes what to expect and how to avoid surprises. It is a must-read for architects,
planners, performing arts groups, educators and anyone who may be considering building or
renovating a theater.

Case Studies in Crowd Management
Chris Kemp, Iain Hill, Mick Upton, Mark Hamilton **£16.95** ISBN 9781904031482
This important work has been compiled from a series of research projects carried out by
the staff of the Centre for Crowd Management and Security Studies at Buckinghamshire
Chilterns University College, and seminar work carried out in Berlin and Groningen with
partner Yourope. It includes case studies, reports and a crowd management safety plan for
a major outdoor rock concert, safe management of rock concerts utilising a triple barrier
safety system and pan-European Health & Safety Issues.

Close Protection – The Softer Skills *Geoffrey Padgham* **£11.95** ISBN 1904031390
This is the first educational book in a new 'Security Series' for Entertainment Technology
Press, and it coincides with the launch of the new 'Protective Security Management'
Foundation Degree at Buckinghamshire Chilterns University College (BCUC). The author
is a former full-career Metropolitan Police Inspector from New Scotland Yard with 27
years' experience of close protection (CP). For 22 of those years he specialised in operations
and senior management duties with the Royalty Protection Department at Buckingham
Palace, followed by five years in the private security industry specialising in CP training
design and delivery. His wealth of protection experience comes across throughout the text,
which incorporates sound advice and exceptional practical guidance, subtly separating fact
from fiction. This publication is an excellent form of reference material for experienced
operatives, students and trainees.

A Comparative Study of Crowd Behaviour at Two Major Music Events
Chris Kemp, Iain Hill, Mick Upton **£7.95** ISBN 1904031250
A compilation of the findings of reports made at two major live music concerts, and in
particular crowd behaviour, which is followed from ingress to egress.

Control Freak *Wayne Howell* **£28.95** ISBN 9781904031550
Control Freak is the second book by Wayne Howell. It provides an in depth study of
DMX512 and the new RDM (Remote Device Management) standards. The book is aimed
at both users and developers and provides a wealth of real world information based on the
author's twenty year experience of lighting control.

Copenhagen Opera House *Richard Brett and John Offord* **£32.00** ISBN 1904031420
Completed in a little over three years, the Copenhagen Opera House opened with a royal gala
performance on 15th January 2005. Built on a spacious brown-field site, the building is a
landmark venue and this book provides the complete technical background story to an opera
house set to become a benchmark for future design and planning. Sixteen chapters by relevant
experts involved with the project cover everything from the planning of the auditorium
and studio stage, the stage engineering, stage lighting and control and architectural lighting
through to acoustic design and sound technology plus technical summaries.

Electrical Safety for Live Events *Marco van Beek* **£16.95** ISBN 1904031285
This title covers electrical safety regulations and good pracitise pertinent to the
entertainment industries and includes some basic electrical theory as well as clarifying the
"do's and don't's" of working with electricity.

Entertainment in Production Volume 1: 1994-1999 *Rob Halliday* **£24.95**
ISBN 9781904031512

Entertainment in Production Volume 2: 2000-2006 *Rob Halliday* **£24.95**
ISBN 9781904031529
Rob Halliday has a dual career as a lighting designer/programmer and author and in these
two volumes he provides the intriguing but comprehensive technical background stories
behind the major musical productions and other notable projects spanning the period 1994 to
2005. Having been closely involved with the majority of the events described, the author is
able to present a first-hand and all-encompassing portrayal of how many of the major shows
across the past decade came into being. From *Oliver!* and *Miss Saigon* to *Mamma Mia!* and
Mary Poppins, here the complete technical story unfolds. The books, which are profusely
illustrated, are in large part an adapted selection of articles that first appeared in the magazine
Lighting&Sound International.

Entertainment Technology Yearbook 2008 *John Offord* **£14.95** ISBN 9781904031543
The new Entertainment Technology Yearbook 2008 covers the year 2007 and includes
picture coverage of major industry exhibitions in Europe compiled from the pages of
Entertainment Technology magazine and the etnow.com website, plus articles and pictures
of production, equipment and project highlights of the year. Also included is a major
European Trade Directory that will be regularly updated on line. A new edition will be
published each year at the ABTT Theatre Show in London in June.

The Exeter Theatre Fire *David Anderson* **£24.95** ISBN 1904031137
This title is a fascinating insight into the events that led up to the disaster at the Theatre Royal,
Exeter, on the night of September 5th 1887. The book details what went wrong, and the
lessons that were learned from the event.

Fading Light – A Year in Retirement *Francis Reid* **£14.95** ISBN 1904031358
Francis Reid, the lighting industry's favourite author, describes a full year in retirement. "Old

age is much more fun than I expected," he says. Fading Light describes visits and experiences to the author's favourite theatres and opera houses, places of relaxation and re-visits to scholarly institutions.

Focus on Lighting Technology *Richard Cadena* **£17.95** ISBN 1904031145
This concise work unravels the mechanics behind modern performance lighting and appeals to designers and technicians alike. Packed with clear, easy-to-read diagrams, the book provides excellent explanations behind the technology of performance lighting.

The Followspot Guide *Nick Mobsby* **£28.95** ISBN 9781904031499
The first in ETP's Equipment Series, Nick Mobsby's Followspot Guide tells you everything you need to know about followspots, from their history through to maintenance and usage. It's pages include a technical specification of 193 followspots from historical to the latest 2007 versions from major manufacturers.

From Ancient Rome to Rock 'n' Roll – a Review of the UK Leisure Security Industry *Mick Upton* **£14.95** ISBN 9781904031505
From stewarding, close protection and crowd management through to his engagement as a senior consultant Mick Upton has been ever present in the events industry. A founder of ShowSec International in 1982 he was its chairman until 2000. The author has led the way on training within the sector. He set up the ShowSec Training Centre and has acted as a consultant at the Bramshill Police College. He has been prominent in the development of courses at Buckinghamshire New University where he was awarded a Doctorate in 2005. Mick has received numerous industry awards. His book is a personal account of the development and professionalism of the sector across the past 50 years.

Health and Safety Aspects in the Live Music Industry *Chris Kemp, Iain Hill* **£30.00** ISBN 1904031226
This title includes chapters on various safety aspects of live event production and is written by specialists in their particular areas of expertise.

Health and Safety Management in the Live Music and Events Industry *Chris Hannam* **£25.95** ISBN 1904031307
This title covers the health and safety regulations and their application regarding all aspects of staging live entertainment events, and is an invaluable manual for production managers and event organisers.

Hearing the Light – 50 Years Backstage *Francis Reid* **£24.95** ISBN 1904031188
This highly enjoyable memoir delves deeply into the theatricality of the industry. The author's almost fanatical interest in opera, his formative period as lighting designer at Glyndebourne and his experiences as a theatre administrator, writer and teacher make for a broad and unique background.

An Introduction to Rigging in the Entertainment Industry *Chris Higgs* **£24.95** ISBN 1904031129
This book is a practical guide to rigging techniques and practices and also thoroughly covers safety issues and discusses the implications of working within recommended guidelines and regulations. Second edition revised September 2008.

Let There be Light – Entertainment Lighting Software Pioneers in Conversation
Robert Bell **£32.00** ISBN 1904031242
Robert Bell interviews a distinguished group of software engineers working on
entertainment lighting ideas and products.

Light and Colour Filters *Michael Hall and Eddie Ruffell* **£23.95** ISBN 9781904031598
Written by two acknowledged and respected experts in the field, this book is destined to
become the standard reference work on the subject. The title chronicles the development
and use of colour filters and also describes how colour is perceived and how filters function.
Up-to-date reference tables will help the practitioner make better and more specific choices
of colour.

Lighting for Roméo and Juliette *John Offord* **£26.95** ISBN 1904031161
John Offord describes the making of the Vienna State Opera production from the lighting
designer's viewpoint – from the point where director Jürgen Flimm made his decision not to
use scenery or sets and simply employ the expertise of LD Patrick Woodroffe.

Lighting Systems for TV Studios *Nick Mobsby* **£45.00** ISBN 1904031005
Lighting Systems for TV Studios, now in its second edition, is the first book specifically
written on the subject and has become the 'standard' resource work for studio planning
and design covering the key elements of system design, luminaires, dimming, control,
data networks and suspension systems as well as detailing the infrastructure items such as
cyclorama, electrical and ventilation. Sensibly TV lighting principles are explained and
some history on TV broadcasting, camera technology and the equipment is provided to
help set the scene! The second edition includes applications for sine wave and distributed
dimming, moving lights, Ethernet and new cool lamp technology.

Lighting Techniques for Theatre-in-the-Round *Jackie Staines* **£24.95** ISBN 1904031013
Lighting Techniques for Theatre-in-the-Round is a unique reference source for those
working on lighting design for theatre-in-the-round for the first time. It is the first title to
be published specifically on the subject, it also provides some anecdotes and ideas for more
challenging shows, and attempts to blow away some of the myths surrounding lighting in
this format.

Lighting the Stage *Francis Reid* **£14.95** ISBN 1904031080
Lighting the Stage discusses the human relationships involved in lighting design – both
between people, and between these people and technology. The book is written from a
highly personal viewpoint and its 'thinking aloud' approach is one that Francis Reid has
used in his writings over the past 30 years.

Model National Standard Conditions *ABTT/DSA/LGLA* **£20.00** ISBN 1904031110
These *Model National Standard Conditions* covers operational matters and complement *The
Technical Standards for Places of Entertainment*, which describes the physical requirements
for building and maintaining entertainment premises.

Mr Phipps' Theatre *Mark Jones, John Pick* **£17.95** ISBN: 1904031382
Mark Jones and John Pick describe "The Sensational Story of Eastbourne's Royal Hip-
podrome" – formerly Eastbourne Theatre Royal. An intriguing narrative, the book sets the
story against a unique social history of the town. Peter Longman, former director of The
Theatres Trust, provides the Foreword.

Pages From Stages *Anthony Field* **£17.95** ISBN 1904031269
Anthony Field explores the changing style of theatres including interior design, exterior design, ticket and seat prices, and levels of service, while questioning whether the theatre still exists as a place of entertainment for regular theatre-goers.

Performing Arts Technical Training Handbook 2009/2010 *ed: John Offord* **£19.95** ISBN 9781904031604
Published in association with the ABTT (Association of British Theatre Technicians), this important Handbook includes fully detailed and indexed entries describing courses on backstage crafts offered by over 100 universities and colleges across the UK. A completely new research project, with accompanying website, the title also includes articles with advice for those considering a career 'behind the scenes', together with contact information and descriptions of the major organisations involved with industry training – plus details of companies offering training within their own premises. The Handbook will be kept in print, with a major revision annually.

Practical Dimming *Nick Mobsby* **£22.95** ISBN 19040313447
This important and easy to read title covers the history of electrical and electronic dimming, how dimmers work, current dimmer types from around the world, planning of a dimming system, looking at new sine wave dimming technology and distributed dimming. Integration of dimming into different performance venues as well as the necessary supporting electrical systems are fully detailed. Significant levels of information are provided on the many different forms and costs of potential solutions as well as how to plan specific solutions. Architectural dimming for the likes of hotels, museums and shopping centres is included. Practical Dimming is a companion book to Practical DMX and is designed for all involved in the use, operation and design of dimming systems.

Practical DMX *Nick Mobsby* **£16.95** ISBN 1904031368
In this highly topical and important title the author details the principles of DMX, how to plan a network, how to choose equipment and cables, with data on products from around the world, and how to install DMX networks for shows and on a permanently installed basis. The easy style of the book and the helpful fault finding tips, together with a review of different DMX testing devices provide an ideal companion for all lighting technicians and system designers. An introduction to Ethernet and Canbus networks are provided as well tips on analogue networks and protocol conversion. This title has been recently updated to include a new chapter on Remote Device Management that became an international standard in Summer 2006.

Practical Guide to Health and Safety in the Entertainment Industry
Marco van Beek **£14.95** ISBN 1904031048
This book is designed to provide a practical approach to Health and Safety within the Live Entertainment and Event industry. It gives industry-pertinent examples, and seeks to break down the myths surrounding Health and Safety.

Production Management *Joe Aveline* **£17.95** ISBN 1904031102
Joe Aveline's book is an in-depth guide to the role of the Production Manager, and includes real-life practical examples and 'Aveline's Fables' – anecdotes of his experiences with real messages behind them.

Rigging for Entertainment: Regulations and Practice *Chris Higgs* **£19.95**
ISBN 1904031218
Continuing where he left off with his highly successful *An Introduction to Rigging in the Entertainment Industry*, Chris Higgs' second title covers the regulations and use of equipment in greater detail.

Rock Solid Ethernet *Wayne Howell* **£24.95** ISBN 1904031293
Although aimed specifically at specifiers, installers and users of entertainment industry systems, this book will give the reader a thorough grounding in all aspects of computer networks, whatever industry they may work in. The inclusion of historical and technical 'sidebars' make for an enjoyable as well as informative read.

Sixty Years of Light Work *Fred Bentham* **£26.95** ISBN 1904031072
This title is an autobiography of one of the great names behind the development of modern stage lighting equipment and techniques.

Sound for the Stage *Patrick Finelli* **£24.95** ISBN 1904031153
Patrick Finelli's thorough manual covering all aspects of live and recorded sound for performance is a complete training course for anyone interested in working in the field of stage sound, and is a must for any student of sound.

Stage Automation *Anton Woodward* **£12.95** ISBN 9781904031567
The purpose of this book is to explain the stage automation techniques used in modern theatre to achieve some of the spectacular visual effects seen in recent years. The book is targeted at automation operators, production managers, theatre technicians, stage engineering machinery manufacturers and theatre engineering students. Topics are covered in sufficient detail to provide an insight into the thought processes that the stage automation engineer has to consider when designing a control system to control stage machinery in a modern theatre. The author has worked on many stage automation projects and developed the award-winning Impressario stage automation system.

Stage Lighting Design in Britain: The Emergence of the Lighting Designer, 1881-1950 *Nigel Morgan* **£17.95** ISBN 190403134X
This book sets out to ascertain the main course of events and the controlling factors that determined the emergence of the theatre lighting designer in Britain, starting with the introduction of incandescent electric light to the stage, and ending at the time of the first public lighting design credits around 1950. The book explores the practitioners, equipment, installations and techniques of lighting design.

Stage Lighting for Theatre Designers *Nigel Morgan* **£17.95** ISBN 1904031196
This is an updated second edition of Nigel Morgan's popular book for students of theatre design – outlining all the techniques of stage lighting design.

Technical Marketing Techniques *David Brooks, Andy Collier, Steve Norman* **£24.95**
ISBN 190403103X
Technical Marketing is a novel concept, recently defined and elaborated by the authors of this book, with business-to-business companies competing in fast developing technical product sectors.

Technical Standards for Places of Entertainment *ABTT/DSA* **£45.00**
ISBN 9781904031536
Technical Standards for Places of Entertainment details the necessary physical standards
required for entertainment venues. New A4 revised edition June 2008.

Theatre Engineering and Stage Machinery *Toshiro Ogawa* **£30.00**
ISBN 9781904031024
Theatre Engineering and Stage Machinery is a unique reference work covering every aspect
of theatrical machinery and stage technology in global terms, and across the complete
historical spectrum. Revised February 2007.

Theatre Lighting in the Age of Gas *Terence Rees* **£24.95** ISBN 190403117X
Entertainment Technology Press has republished this valuable historic work previously
produced by the Society for Theatre Research in 1978. *Theatre Lighting in the Age of Gas*
investigates the technological and artistic achievements of theatre lighting engineers from
the 1700s to the late Victorian period.

Theatre Space: A Rediscovery Reported *Francis Reid* **£19.95** ISBN 1904031439
In the post-war world of the 1950s and 60s, the format of theatre space became a matter for
a debate that aroused passions of an intensity unknown before or since. The proscenium
arch was clearly identified as the enemy, accused of forming a barrier to disrupt the relations
between the actor and audience. An uneasy fellow-traveller at the time, Francis Reid later
recorded his impressions whilst enjoying performances or working in theatres old and new
and this book is an important collection of his writings in various theatrical journals from
1969-2001 including his contribution to the Cambridge Guide to the Theatre in 1988. It
reports some of the flavour of the period when theatre architecture was rediscovering its past
in a search to establish its future.

Theatres of Achievement *John Higgins* **£29.95** ISBN: 1904031374
John Higgins affectionately describes the history of 40 distinguished UK theatres in a
personal tribute, each uniquely illustrated by the author. Completing each profile is colour
photography by Adrian Eggleston.

Theatric Tourist *Francis Reid* **£19.95** ISBN 9781904031468
Theatric Tourist is the delightful story of Francis Reid's visits across more than 50 years
to theatres, theatre museums, performances and even movie theme parks. In his inimi-
table style, the author involves the reader within a personal experience of venues from
the Legacy of Rome to theatres of the Renaissance and Eighteenth Century Baroque and
the Gustavian Theatres of Stockholm. His performance experiences include Wagner in
Beyreuth, the Pleasures of Tivoli and Wayang in Singapore. This is a 'must have' title for
those who are as "incurably stagestruck" as the author.

Through the Viewfinder *Jeremy Hoare* **£21.95** ISBN: 9781904031574
Do you want to be a top television cameraman? Well this is going to help!
Through the Viewfinder is aimed at media students wanting to be top professional television
cameramen – but it will also be of interest to anyone who wants to know what goes on
behind the cameras that bring so much into our homes.
The author takes his own opinionated look at how to operate a television camera based on
23 years' experience looking through many viewfinders for a major ITV network company.
Based on interviews with people he has worked with, all leaders in the profession, the book

is based on their views and opinions and is a highly revealing portrait of what happens behind the scenes in television production from a cameraman's point of view.

Walt Disney Concert Hall – The Backstage Story *Patricia MacKay & Richard Pilbrow* **£28.95** ISBN 1904031234
Spanning the 16-year history of the design and construction of the Walt Disney Concert Hall, this book provides a fresh and detailed behind the scenes story of the design and technology from a variety of viewpoints. This is the first book to reveal the "process" of the design of a concert hall.

Yesterday's Lights – A Revolution Reported *Francis Reid* **£26.95** ISBN 1904031323
Set to help new generations to be aware of where the art and science of theatre lighting is coming from – and stimulate a nostalgia trip for those who lived through the period, Francis Reid's latest book has over 350 pages dedicated to the task, covering the 'revolution' from the fifties through to the present day. Although this is a highly personal account of the development of lighting design and technology and he admits that there are 'gaps', you'd be hard put to find anything of significance missing.

Go to www.etbooks.co.uk for full details of above titles and secure online ordering facilities.